GARDEN PLANTS
FOR
CONNOISSEURS

This book is dedicated to the gardeners, nurserymen, hybridizers and those with a keen eye who, over the years, have grown or made available new, unusual and otherwise desirable plants for the benefit of the gardening public.

GARDEN PLANTS FOR CONNOISSEURS

Roy Lancaster

TIMBER PRESS
Portland, Oregon

First published in Great Britain by Unwin Hyman, an imprint of Unwin Hyman
Limited, 1987

UNWIN HYMAN LIMITED
Denmark House, 37–39 Queen Elizabeth Street,
London SE1 2QB
and 40 Museum Street, London WC1A 1LU

First published in North America
in 1987 by Timber Press, Inc.,
9999 S.W. Wilshire, Portland,
Oregon 97225, U.S.A.

ISBN 0-88192-088-6

Designed by Julian Holland

Typeset by Latimer Trend & Company Ltd, Plymouth

Printed in Portugal by
Printer Portugesa

Acknowledgements

I am indebted to a number of friends and colleagues in writing this
book. Most important is my wife Sue who, whilst coping with the
demands of a young family, typed my hand-written manuscript and
despite their complaints of 'not another book, Daddy', Edward and
Holly have been more understanding than I had expected. Richard
Cawthorne, Jim Gardiner, David Mason, Graham Pattison, Tony
Schilling, Paul Meyer and Michael Taylor have responded to my
requests for specific information and Dr Elizabeth Schultz and Peter
Wharton have provided information on plant hardiness zones in North
America.

Peter Chappell and Brian Humphrey provided the propagation
details while David Hutchinson (*Rosa bracteata* and *Sorbus cashmiriana*)
and Tony Murdoch (*Magnolia campbellii*) kindly produced wanted
illustrations, the remainder are my own. My kind neighbours Alan and
Doreen Birtwistle, in addition to allowing their garden to be used as an
overflow nursery to my own, also supplied me with scrap paper on
which to scribble my manuscript.

Last but not least are my editor Emma Callery as well as Barry
Ambrose and Faith Whiten who sparked the idea. To all of these I
extend my warm thanks. If I have forgotten inadvertently other help
given me on this project I offer my sincere apologies.

Contents

Foreword

According to my dictionary a connoisseur is a critical judge in matters of taste. When I was invited, therefore, to write a book on garden plants for the connoisseur I decided that such a title was altogether too presumptuous for my liking and I was inclined to say no. I was then asked to write about 100 of my favourite plants and to suggest an alternative title. The idea appealed and I suggested as possible titles *Plants for the Keen Gardener* or *Plantsman's Plants*. As neither of these or others proved acceptable I somewhat reluctantly agreed to write under the original title, consoling myself that readers would soon realize that while I am not easily fooled by 'wolves in sheep's clothing' my tastes in plants are, to put it mildly, catholic.

As for restricting my selection to 100, that was the hard part. It was Will Ingwersen, I believe, who, on being asked to name his ten favourite Alpines replied that he would name his 100 ten favourites. Any keen gardener of experience could cheerfully name hundreds of favourite plants, 100 being a drop in the ocean. As to choice of plants, ask any ten plantspeople to name 100 of their favourites and you can take it for granted that their selections will vary, probably greatly so. Ask me to name my 100 favourites in five growing years from now and as likely as not my list will not entirely agree with the present selection. While some plants remain special favourites throughout one's lifetime others are usurped by newcomers with more attractive credentials. In other words, I should be very surprised indeed to hear of anyone fully concurring with my choice. 'Why on earth did he include that?' will inevitably be a common response.

I grow many of the plants in this book in my garden in Hampshire, mainly on an acid Bagshot sand though some pockets of clay enable me to grow those plants requiring cooler, moister conditions. I brought a good number of them from my previous garden on the shallow chalk soil of Winchester only five miles away. Some of these plants I would always grow in my garden wherever I lived. Like old friends they are reassuring in the way they are always there when needed. Reliable too, in their hardiness and adaptability to different soils and aspects.

My selection also includes plants I have admired in other's gardens and determined to acquire one day for my own. Other plants, either for lack of space or suitable conditions, I cannot hope to grow in my present garden but this does not prevent them from appearing in this book.

A good number of these plants I have also seen in the wild state a useful experience in that it helps one to understand their requirements in cultivation. From an availability point of view, most of the plants described are readily obtainable from several sources at least, while others will need searching for. Just a few are, to my knowledge, not presently available in commerce though they may well be represented in specialist collections or famous gardens. It is my belief that there is nothing in the following selection beyond the reach of the diligent and patient gardener.

Introduction

It is a common practice when writing books about ornamental plants to include short chapters on general cultivation, pests and diseases and propagation. Bearing in mind the level of expertise and experience implied by the title *Garden Plants for Connoisseurs* I decided not to waste valuable space in this account on a reiteration of basic principles such as how to plant and care for a tree, the benefits of mulching and feeding and of soil improvement in general. Much of this is based on common sense and has been discussed in countless articles and books over the years. Where relevant, however, I have referred to specific details of cultivation in my accounts of individual plants.

Pests and diseases have never been my strong point and I do not mind admitting it. It is a subject on which I have dwelt only when forced to though I readily accept its importance in a gardener's education. Like most gardeners, I have suffered my share of frustration and misfortunes at the hands of honey fungus, verticillium wilt, slugs, red spider mite and sundry other nasties and, like fishermen, I have a store of experiences concerning my exploits in attempting to curb, if not end, their activities. When faced with a new or unfamiliar pest, disease or disorder in my garden I seek the advice of others more familiar and involved with these subjects or by consulting the plethora of leaflets, guides and books readily available in bookshops, garden centres and libraries.

Most keen gardeners like to try producing their own plants from seed, cuttings or by division and particularly in the case of rare or semi-hardy plants this practice is to be encouraged. For those whose experience of propagation is limited or nil there are a number of first class books on the subject available, not all of which are technical or expensive. In addition, gardeners have ready access to such information, demonstrations even through membership of one of the growing number of conservation orientated plant societies and groups which are presently springing up all over Britain.

References in the text to means of increase are principally aimed at alerting readers to possible reasons for a plant's rarity in cultivation, eg, *Paeonia suffruticosa* 'Joseph Rock' and *Lathraea clandestina*. The emphasis on nurserymen in this connection is deliberate. Despite the natural inclination among keen gardeners to propagate their own stock, they should remember that most nurserymen are also keen plantsmen and women, not in business solely for the profit. Both gardeners and plant hunters owe a great debt of gratitude to nurserymen who have worked all hours using hard-earned skills and experience and taken financial risks in establishing new plants in cultivation and making them available to the public. There have been nurserymen more interested in their plants than their profits who have suffered as a result. Some such are still around and considering their over-riding desire to please their customers with quality plants at reasonable cost they deserve all the support the gardening public can give them.

On the question of publicizing plants by writing about them or otherwise drawing the public's attention to them in the media, there are two main schools of thought. On the one hand there are those holding the opinion that unless a plant is guaranteed available in the nursery trade then it is best left well alone on the basis that what the eye

Magnolia *'Heaven Scent'* – a beautiful American-raised tree magnolia. The Hillier Arboretum, Hampshire (April).

does not read or hear about the heart will not grieve after. To be excited by news of a new or rare plant only to find it unavailable some people feel is an unnecessary disappointment and one which should at all costs be avoided. After all, they reason, there is no shortage of good plants on the market and those that are not around at present will no doubt make their appearance one day.

While I can sympathize with this point of view I have talked with enough keen gardeners over the years to know that the apparent unavailability of a desirable plant generally makes them all the keener to have it. This brings me to another important point in the argument, that is, which comes first – supply or demand? Is the onus on the nurseryman to make a little known or new plant available to the public or is it up to the gardening public to indicate its interest by placing firm orders? I well recall the late Sir Harold Hillier writing the following note for *Hillier's Manual of Trees and Shrubs* in 1970 – 'A number of rare items have been included of which we may have no immediately available stock, but it is hoped that we shall be in a position to offer these in the near future. With rare or little known plants we rely on public demand to justify propagation.'

This plea would, I am sure, be voiced by many nurserymen and women today. Since the days of the 'big nurseries' dominating the market for new and little known plants, a host of smaller concerns have become established some of which are specializing in given families, genera or even specific groups. Although the remaining large nurseries still offer a vast selection of plants between them, the input from these smaller nurseries has greatly increased both the range and availability of the rare and the unusual. This is naturally good news to keen gardeners and plant enthusiasts since it increases the likelihood of obtaining desired treasures. Far from irritating the reader, I hope that my inclusion in this book of a few plants not immediately available will encourage them to explore every channel in making them available at the earliest opportunity.

I have saved until last what many believe to be the most hazardous aspect of writing on plants. Here, my brief to keep in mind the interests of gardeners in Britain and in North America is on dangerous ground indeed. As an English gardener and plantsman I am aware of the great variety of climatic conditions experienced in the British Isles. While fairly confident statements can be made about major climatic features such as the relative wetter conditions of western Britain and the drier conditions of eastern Britain, it is when one comes to detail that the trouble begins, especially when it concerns winter hardiness. Again, it might be said that southern and south-western areas of Britain are generally milder than the north and east and therefore are most suitable for growing the less hardy plants out of doors but this does not mean that such plants are not worth attempting elsewhere. Such are the idiosyncracies of local weather patterns that tender plants are sometimes successful in parts of Britain well outside the so-called 'soft south'.

The distribution of such plants in British cultivation is also affected by the presence of micro climates which are often so local as to exist in one garden and not the next or even in one corner of a garden and not in another. Only by observation and experiment can keen gardeners exploit the conditions peculiar to their gardens.

Adding to the complexity of the British climate are the changes that appear to be taking place. After a period of several years when relatively mild winters have enabled the cultivation of a wide range of plants from Mediterranean climates, recent winters have brought severe conditions such as have not been experienced in living memory. For the past three winters, freezing winds and plummetting temperatures have caused devastation in gardens over much of Britain including the so-called mild areas of the south-west and west. As a result, recommending plants which are sure to be hardy in certain areas has become a hazardous business with few guarantees.

When it comes to the North American climate, the problems set by Britain are magnified a hundredfold and any British horticulturalist who attempts to treat it in detail is either brave or foolhardy. My limited experience of American conditions persuades me to decline but not to ignore the challenge. Of course, I have learned enough on my travels to recognize that certain areas are more favourable to certain plants than others. Every state has its contrasts and variations and I can think of no better example than California where in different gardens one can grow desert plants, subtropical plants and plants from the cool temperate zones, to quote just three examples.

Of course, on the basis of 'where there's a will there's a way' gardeners can often provide artificial conditions conducive to the cultivation of specific plants. Unfortunately these are often anything but permanent or satisfactory but if they serve a purpose and give pleasure then who can complain? I have often seen camellias grown in prepared peat beds raised above the native alkaline soil. If thoroughly prepared and cared for they can be highly successful bringing years of enjoyment and satisfaction whereas those erected in a hurry often bring disappointment if not disenchantment. One of the most successful examples of artificially induced conditions I have ever seen is in the woodland garden of Harold Epstein at La Rochelle, New York where an overhead irrigation system provides just the right amount of moisture at the critical times to enable a wealth of choice plants to flourish. During the long drought of 1985, Harold's sprinklers attached to the stems of selected trees played a vital part in ensuring the survival of many of his most precious perennials.

The above system affected almost an entire garden while another much simpler device I once saw in an English garden used to encourage the growth of just one plant, *Lapageria rosea*. A native of the Chilean rain forests, this climber was flourishing in a relatively dry garden because the owner had planted it on a north wall against a badly cracked rainpipe which drained water from the roof. During rains, water seeping through the crack which extended almost the entire length of the pipe provided just the right conditions for the lapageria which covered the pipe in a rich leafy embrace. Hopefully, readers will take the above points into account when noting my comments relating to hardiness and growing conditions.

For the rest of the text, it is a mixture of personal experience of plants growing in the wild and in cultivation spiced with the occasional observation from other, far wiser, gardeners. The mark of a keen gardener is that he or she is game to try any plant within reason. It is on this basis that the following selection was chosen. If, despite the pitfalls and potential disappointments associated with growing rare or difficult plants, the gardener succeeds in growing a plant encountered for the first time in this book I shall be well pleased. In addition, if its cultivation brings anything like the amount of pleasure these plants have brought to me then I shall consider my efforts well spent. Happy hunting!

Trees

Acer griseum

Acer griseum – superb, rich brown peeling bark. Hillier's West Hill Nursery, Winchester (July).

On a warm June day in 1910 the famous English plant hunter E. H. ('Chinese') Wilson was following a tortuous track up a mountainside in China's Hubei province. Wilson and his heavily loaded porters climbed to a gap in the ridge before descending at breakneck speed the other side. The slopes were densely clothed with trees and lesser vegetation and Wilson, not suprisingly, made several stops in order to examine the many interesting and ornamental plants flanking the track. He found a new poplar with bronze-red young foliage, a rose-violet flowered primula and a new hydrangea with huge flannel-like leaves which was later named *Hydrangea sargentiana* after his employer Charles Sargent of the Arnold Arboretum, Massachusetts, USA. He also found a tree with rich reddish-brown, peeling bark—*Acer griseum*.

It was not the first time he had seen this lovely maple. Indeed, he had made the first collection of its seed nine years earlier on his very first expedition for the English Nursery firm of James Veitch & Sons of Chelsea. However, they were not able to include this tree in their autumn catalogue until 1912. From the day it was made available to the gardening public, the Chinese Paper-bark Maple, as it became known, was assured of a permanent place in our gardens and it remains one of the most desirable and distinguished of all maples, if not all trees.

It is not a large tree by most standards, and its relatively slow growth makes it suitable for all but the smallest gardens. Indeed, if only one tree could be accommodated in the garden then *Acer griseum* must be a strong candidate. Given time, a moist but well drained soil and a sheltered position it is capable of reaching 10m (32ft) or more in height. Wilson reported trees of 18m (60ft) in China but it is doubtful if any large trees still exist there as this maple has been widely cut in the wild where its status is rare if not endangered.

The bark, which is the most outstanding feature of this tree, has been variously described as rich brown, coppery brown and cinnamon-red (Wilson's own description). It is paper-thin and when old, peels away to reveal the richer-coloured young bark beneath. It is particularly peely on the branches especially at their junctions with the main stem where it often collects in dense, loose bunches.

In leaf, *A. griseum* differs from most maples in having three leaflets, like those of a clover. These are boldly toothed, green above and a contrasting bluish-grey beneath, hence the Latin name *griseum* meaning 'grey'. These colour red or orange in autumn before falling. The drooping clusters of red flowers are relatively insignificant and are followed by downy, typically winged fruits. Although free fruiting in cultivation, many of the fruits are without seeds (kernels), or if these are present, they are often undeveloped and therefore infertile. This is the main reason why *Acer griseum* is not as common in cultivation as its merit would suggest. Occasional specimens are found which bear a high proportion of fertile seed and such trees are naturally like gold mines to the nurseryman.

Relatively unfussed as to soil, I have seen this tree thriving equally on moderately acid and alkaline soils but it does not like badly drained situations or cold exposed sites. It is, however, a hardy tree and handsome examples can be found in most cool temperate areas, except perhaps in the far north. An established tree, when well grown and well sited is a joy to behold, especially when used as a focal point. It is particularly impressive when viewed against snow which acts as a perfect foil. It comes very close to being an 'all rounder' since its rounded crown and neatly attractive leaves give it a pleasing aspect in summer and its red and orange autumn foliage leaves a lasting impression. Throughout the year, the bark is highly ornamental, taking on a special significance in winter when, unimpeded by leaves it shines with a rare allure.

Acer 'Silver Vein'

After the Japanese maples, which are grown mainly for their fine foliage and autumn tints, one of the most popular groups of ornamental acers are the snake bark maples so-called because of the white, pale green or grey vertical striations which give the thin bark its characteristic appearance. Which particular snake, if any, the comparison has in mind I have yet to discover but this in no way detracts from the importance of these trees in our gardens. The first 'snake bark' to be introduced to western cultivation in 1755 was the moosewood – *Acer pensylvanicum* which despite its descriptive Latin name meaning 'of Pennsylvania', is found over several states and provinces of eastern North America as far south as Georgia. It grows there in rich, moist woodlands and I shall never forget my first encounter with this maple several years ago on a wooded hillside above St. Adel, north of Montreal in Quebec. The only way I could progress through the wood was to use the slender stems of this maple to pull me up the steep slope. Moosewood was plentiful here as an understorey and its striped stems (it is sometimes called the Striped Maple) helped lighten the shade of the canopy.

Acer 'Silver Vein' – striking 'snake bark' effects. Original seedling. The Hillier Arboretum, Hampshire (November).

The moosewood is hardy and easy in cultivation reaching on average 4.5 to 6m (15 to 20ft) but capable of 9m (30ft) or more under ideal conditions, especially in woodland. It develops a vase-shaped habit with steeply ascending branches that arch towards their tips, eventually forming a rather flat-topped or rounded crown. The leaves are fairly large, up to 18cm (7in) long on young trees. In shape they broaden from the heart-shaped base into three, bold pointed lobes and in colour they are a matt green, pink tinged on emerging and changing in autumn to a rich yellow when they shine in the slanting rays of the sun.

Unlike the Paper-bark Maple, the moosewood is a relatively fast grower – 6m (20ft) after only 12 years in ideal conditions. It thrives best on neutral to moderately acid soil and although naturally shade tolerant, it is best grown as a specimen in an open situation where its bark characteristics can best be seen and appreciated.

Among other snake bark maples, the Chinese *Acer davidii* is one of the most frequently planted. It is named after French missionary Armand David who sent specimens of it to Paris in 1869. It is, however, a widely distributed maple in the wild and its seed has been introduced by several plant collectors from various provinces of central and western China. These introductions have continued to the present day and as I write this note I can see through my study window a flourishing specimen in my garden grown from seed collected as recently as 1980 on sacred Emei Shan, a mountain in Sichuan province.

Compared with the American moosewood, *Acer davidii* tends to be a freer growing tree with more numerous, widely spreading branches and smaller leaves usually without lobes. Naturally, with such a wide distribution in the wild it varies in minor details and one of these variations, grown from seed introduced by the Scottish plant hunter George Forrest has been given the collector's name *Acer davidii* 'George Forrest'. This is an exceptional maple with boldly arching stems and glossy deep green leaves borne on rhubarb-red stalks. Even the shoots are reddish and polished and are at their most attractive in winter.

It might be thought that with two maples such as these there could not possibly be room in a garden for any other snake barks, but this is not so. In the late spring of 1959 or 1960 in the Chandlers Ford, Hampshire nursery of Messrs Hilliers a deliberate hybrid was induced by placing the pollen of *Acer pensylvanicum* 'Erythrocladum' (a form with coral red young stems in winter) onto the flowers of a maple then labelled *Acer laxiflorum* but more likely a form of *Acer davidii*, possibly 'George Forrest'. The cross was made by a Dutchman, Peter Douwsma, who was then employed as an assistant propagator. From this interesting cross, four seedlings were produced one of which, the best, was subsequently given the name 'Silver Vein' from the silvery striations present on the bark. These are especially noticeable in winter when they give to the bark a 'bloomy' appearance. In most characters, 'Silver Vein' is intermediate between its parents, embodying the best of both. It is vase-shaped at first, later spreading widely with arching tips and dark reddish young shoots.

The leaves are larger than those of *A. davidii* and favour more the American parent in shape. In autumn, the leaves predictably turn a rich yellow and when shed, form a golden carpet on the ground beneath. Unlike *A. davidii* and *A. pensylvanicum* which are normally seed grown, 'Silver Vein' is propagated by grafting which has limited its distribution in cultivation. Nevertheless, it is available now from several sources, in Britain certainly, and is a tree worth hunting for. Its ultimate size is likely to be that of *A. pensylvanicum* and it should be given space in which to develop its natural habit.

Acer triflorum

While few people would deny *Acer griseum* the crown for ornamental bark, there is another maple which, in the opinion of some gardeners, runs it a close second. This is *Acer triflorum*, the name referring to its flowers, carried in clusters of three. The leaves too, are composed of three leaflets which bear irregular teeth and scattered hairs. Like *Acer griseum*, it is hardy and relatively slow in growth with an attractive rounded or oval crown which makes it a suitable choice for all but the smallest gardens.

The peeling bark, while not as pronounced as that of *A. griseum*, is distinct enough to persuade one to take a closer look. In colour it is a dark cinnamon red, peeling in vertical strips. On the main stem and major branches the mature bark is ash brown, rich and loose with strong vertical fissures. As a winter feature, it is excellent, deserving of the same treatment by way of conditions and siting as its more well-known relative. Its supreme moment, however, arrives with autumn when the leaves exhibit rich yellow, red or orange tints, intensifying daily until the whole canopy glows like a bright bonfire. Young

Acer triflorum – *young tree showing typical autumn leaf effects. The Hillier Arboretum, Hampshire (October).*

specimens colour well, too, and not even the much vaunted Japanese maples can challenge its brilliance.

In the wild, *A. triflorum* is native to Korea and north-east China where it is often found with other deciduous trees rubbing shoulders with dark, evergreen pines and firs against which its autumn blaze can be electrifying. Strangely, although it was seen and described by E. H. Wilson in North Korea around 1917, another eight years passed before its successful introduction into western cultivation where it is still relatively unknown. In the wild, according to Wilson, trees up to 27m (80ft) are known, but specimens half this height are the norm.

When it comes to propagation, *A. triflorum* has much the same characteristics as that of *A. griseum*. It can, however, be propagated by grafting and has even been grown from cuttings.

Aesculus californica

To those brought up with the familiar bulk of the village-green horse chestnut, it comes as a bit of a surprise to meet its Californian cousin the California Buckeye. Although *Aesculus californica* is capable in certain situations in the wild of reaching 12m (40ft), it is most commonly seen as a short-stemmed tree or large bush rarely more than 4.5m (15ft) high

Aesculus californica – flowering tree with typically broad low crown. Bath Botanic Garden, Avon (July).

and as much or more across. Old specimens often develop a flaking bark on the main stem. Its summer aspect is dense and leafy, the leaves five to seven fingered and of a distinctive glossy metallic green.

I first saw *A. californica* in Bath, Avon where an impressive specimen grows, or used to grow, in the Botanic Garden there. It was in July 1977 and the tree was in full flower, the erect cylindrical heads of white flowers rising from the tips of almost every other shoot. Only on closer examination did I recognize it to be a kind of buckeye. The individual flowers sometimes have a pink stain in the throat while the long stamens with orange anthers are thrust beyond the petals adding considerably to the overall effect.

I have seen this tree in several gardens and parks since and although hardy, there is no doubting that it enjoys plenty of sun and a well drained position in order to thrive. It flowers best during a warm summer which is not surprising considering its homeland from whence it was originally introduced by the Cornish plant collector William Lobb in 1850. In October 1985, I saw it growing wild in the coastal ranges east of San Francisco where it is a common member of the dense scrub (chaparral) on dry slopes and in canyons. It shares its territory with a host of evergreen and often thorny shrubs including buckthorns, ceanothus, arctostaphylos and oaks. Among these, the buckeye stood out a mile and there was no mistaking its identity. For a start, it was already bare of leaves so that the grey white of its branches shone ghostlike in the unremitting sun. On closer examination, we found the branches to be strung with large fig-shaped fruits which hung like baubles on long brown stalks. Some of the spineless, green, fruit cases were already splitting to reveal a pale brown seed though the majority ripen to a striking orange-brown before releasing their charges. The

mature seed of the California Buckeye has to be seen to be believed. It is a conker player's dream come true. Some that I collected were 7.5cm (3in) across and quite weighty, of a dark polished brown.

Aesculus californica – *pale branches of wild tree in autumn. Sierra Nevada, California (October).*

This buckeye germinates well from seed when it is obtainable, otherwise nurserymen must resort to grafting as a means of increase. The best specimens I have seen in cultivation have been encouraged to develop a main stem which means planting them in their permanent site as young as possible. In Britain, the California Buckeye is rarely as free fruiting as it is in the wild nor do its branches display quite the same bleached appearance – a result of regular sun and dry conditions. It is, however, a well-shaped flowering tree ideally suited to an isolated position in a lawn or bed with room to grow to its maximum proportions.

The leaves are normally shed earlier than most, a survival mechanism which, in the wild helps reduce stress in drought situations. This characteristic can be put to good use in cultivation, especially where a small tree is required for an artificially dry environment such as a large courtyard or an inner city development.

Alnus firma

I first noticed this alder on a winter's visit to Kew Gardens. Being a deciduous tree, it was its naked crown that first caught my eye and it possessed a certain grace and elegance of branching not normally associated with alders. More than anything else, however, I was attracted to the bark of its main stem. In the pale sunlight, it had a dappled effect caused by the grey or green tinted old bark flaking away

Above: Alnus firma – *attractive bark of old tree in winter. Royal Botanic Gardens, Kew (March).*
Below: Alnus pendula – *beautifully veined and tapered leaves. Hergest Croft, Herefordshire (August).*

in thick, irregularly shaped fragments to reveal the warm brown, new bark beneath. In a hardy tree this mixture of ruggedness and grace is most uncommon and when this is combined with an impressive leaf, such as those of *A. firma*, one is confronted with a tree of unusual character.

The leaf has been likened to that of a hornbeam but much as I admire the latter and its foliage, it pales in comparison to this alder. The fresh-green leaves of *Alnus firma* which, as the name suggest are firm in texture, can be as much as 11.5cm (4½in) long and less than half as much wide with numerous impressed parallel veins and edged with fine teeth. It is the veins which make the leaf so unforgettable and poised as the leaves are, along slender arching shoots, they present a picture of great elegance.

Even more elegant and desirable is *Alnus pendula*, a related species, which is unfortunately still rare and virtually unobtainable commercially in western cultivation. It is sometimes classed as a variety of *A. firma* under the name *A. firma* var. *multinervis* but differs amongst other things in its leaves which are longer, narrower and more slender pointed with more numerous veins. They are borne along shoots which, despite the name, are more arching than weeping, except in old specimens. An established plant growing at Hergest Croft in Herefordshire is more shrub than tree with a broad, low crown of slender branches like a green waterfall. With care young plants could no doubt be trained on a single stem to form a charming 'weeping' tree.

Like *A. pendula*, *Alnus firma* is a native of Japan where it is widespread in the mountains and variable in habit and leaf. The typical form is said to be shrubby while the form common on the main island is a downy leaved tree known as forma *hirtella*. This is the form normally seen in western cultivation. It was first introduced in the 1890s and the tree described above is one of two planted at Kew in 1893. This tree is approximately 12.2m (40ft) high and thriving.

The male catkins appear with the young leaves in the spring unlike those of most other alders which are formed the previous summer. Although small compared with some, they are bright gold in colour and produced in great numbers. Nurserymen propagate this tree either by seed (when obtainable) or by cuttings. Tolerant of most soils and situations, it is hard to understand why this under-rated tree in its hardier forms is so uncommon in cultivation.

Aralia elata 'Variegata'

Almost the first botanical name I learned as a young man was *Aralia elata*. It belonged to a peculiar looking tree which grew in a shrubbery in the Lancashire park where I first began my gardening career. It was peculiar to my then inexperienced eyes for its stems were stout and pithy and beset with thorns. These were scattered on mature stems but densely set and positively hostile on the sucker growths which abounded wherever old stems had been damaged or cut down. I had discovered the Angelica tree, as it is also known, on a grey winter's day when its straight, few branched stems to 3.5m (12ft) tall looked as lifeless as the fork with which I laboured on the soil beneath. How wrong I was. In spring, the seemingly moribund buds which studded the stems burst open to release leaves lush and subtropical in their ultimate expanse. *Aralia elata* was, for me, a revelation which did not

Aralia elata 'Variegata' – typical low domed crown of old tree. Knightshayes Court, Devon (September).

end with the foliage, handsome though this was, for late in the year from the tip of each stem and major branch rose a large, loose flower-head comprising a myriad tiny, creamy-white flowers. These appeared to attract all the insects in the neighbourhood though I could detect no noticeable scent.

Since that first introduction, I have seen the Angelica tree on many occasions in a wide range of situations and my admiration for it as a hardy ornamental tree or large shrub has steadily increased. Its credentials are impressive. It grows to 3.5 or 4.75m (12 or 15ft) on average but is capable of twice this in a sheltered or woodland situation. Its wide-spreading crown can in time, expand to 7m (20ft) or more across, especially if it is encouraged to branch from close to the base.

Because of the proliferation of buds along the stems, specimens can become dense and bushy if left unchecked and it is sometimes advisable to prune away the lower growths to encourage a single stem with an elevated crown. Such trees are more easily accommodated in smaller gardens where part of the spread is carried over a boundary wall, hedge or fence. Indeed, in smaller gardens it can be trained to form a small tree or shrub to 2.5 or 3.5m (8 to 10ft) by judicious pruning, but one must then beware the resultant suckers.

In those gardens where space is no problem, the Angelica tree is seen at its best, developing in time to give a broad, often dome-shaped, crown. The leaves are deeply divided into numerous leaflets not unlike those of the common Angelica (*Angelica archangelica*) and can be 1m (3ft) or more long. They are among the largest leaves of any hardy tree and bring a touch of the exotic to otherwise ordinary gardens. The flowers which appear in late summer are replaced – if the summer has been warm – by tiny, purplish-black, berry-like fruits which hang in heavy bunches, often after leaf fall.

It is, generally speaking, a hardy tree, although in rich soils unripened stems are subject to damage in severe winters. Such damage is normally replaced the following spring by suckers from below ground, however. It is usually amenable to most soils excepting those subject to waterlogging and because of its architectural qualities of habit and leaf it associates well with buildings as well as making a handsome lawn specimen. It is especially useful in city gardens where it appears untroubled by pollution and if it has one minus point it is the alacrity with which it produces suckers which might prove a nuisance. On the other hand, they are easily lifted in winter and make useful presents for gardening friends.

In the wild, *Aralia elata* is found in Korea, east Siberia, Japan and north-east China where it frequents thickets, hillside scrub and forest margins. It was first introduced around 1830 and again on several occasions since. It is available, though not as commonly as its merit deserves, from specialist growers who propagate it from root cuttings, suckers or by seed. There are also two splendid, though slower-growing variegated forms, in 'Variegata', which has grey-green leaflets irregularly margined with creamy white, and 'Aureo-variegata'. In this form, the leaflets are margined golden-yellow at first, paling to cream later. Both variegated forms are occasionally available from specialist growers who propagate them by grafting onto stocks of the green type. Though slow to mature and prone to producing green-leaved suckers which must be removed, these two make striking specimens in time and are well worth the trouble.

Arbutus x andrachnoides

The so-called Strawberry trees (*Arbutus* species), are a relatively small group of evergreen ornamentals in the British Isles, several of which are not winter hardy. The most commonly cultivated member of this group is the Killarney Strawberry Tree, *A. unedo*, which is hardy in warm areas of the cool temperate zones. Even so, its foliage can be scorched and its shoots killed back in unusually severe winters, especially when the wind-chill factor sends temperatures plummeting.

The name Strawberry Tree is derived from the colour and size of the fruits which, however, are far removed from the strawberry in taste and texture. Interestingly, these fruits, which are rounded and warty, take a whole year to ripen so that they are at their most colourful when the next year's flowers are in bloom. The drooping clusters of red fruits and the nodding white, pitcher-shaped flowers (pink tinted in 'Rubra') together provide a pleasing combination and remain so until hungry birds remove the fruits. The bark of *A. unedo* is dark and fibrous while the leaves are toothed and of a dark shining green.

A curious fact about this tree is that even though it is a member of the rhododendron family (*Ericaceae*), it is not averse to lime in the soil and is commonly seen growing in gardens in chalk or limestone

Arbutus × andrachnoides – *handsome
evergreen with richly coloured bark.
Jenkyn Place, Hampshire (July).*

country. It is, of course, just as happy – if not more so – on acid soils
and anyone who has seen this tree on the islands and shores of the Lakes
of Killarney in Co. Kerry will be in no doubt about this.

Apart from south-west Ireland, *A. unedo* also occurs wild in Brittany
in France and the Mediterranean region. Towards the eastern end of its
range, especially in south-east Europe, it is often found growing with
another species *A. andrachne*, sometimes referred to as the Greek
Strawberry Tree. Although this tree was first introduced to Britain as
long ago as 1724, it remains very rare. Not surprisingly, considering its
homeland, it has a craving for sun and warmth and the first specimens I
ever saw in cultivation grew in the University Botanic Garden,
Cambridge, in the comparatively drier climate of East Anglia.

In the hills of Greece, east of the Pindus Range, I saw this tree in 1974
growing on steep rocky slopes, while some gnarled specimens even
grew in fissures in the rock itself. It was a low tree there, no more than
6m (20ft) sharing its territory with the Bladder Senna (*Colutea
arborescens*) and the Venetian Sumach (*Cotinus coggygria*). I was immediately struck by the rich oxblood red of its old bark which flaked
away to expose a pale pea-green, young bark. Indeed, the young bark

on some stems was bleached almost white by the sun. It looked to be 'light years' removed from the Killarney Strawberry Tree but the two mix quite freely in some locations (I saw them sharing the same slopes in the Meteora district) and where they do so, hybrids may occur.

Considering that *A. unedo* is in flower from late autumn to early winter and those of *A. andrachne* in the spring, one assumes that only when late flowers of the former and early flowers of the latter coincide can such an event as hybridizing take place. The resultant hybrids bear the name *A.x andrachnoides* – meaning 'like *Arbutus andrachne*' – and are not uncommon in cultivation, in Britain certainly. One of the finest, despite winter damage in recent years, still grows at Bodnant Gardens in North Wales while others may be found at Highdown Gardens, Nr. Shoreham in Sussex and in Battersea Park, London. When last measured in 1983, the last named was 14m (46ft) tall.

I first came across this tree at the Cambridge Botanic Garden but an even finer one grew on the shallow chalk soil of Hilliers Nursery in Winchester when I first arrived to work there in 1962. Typically, this was broader than high and its smooth barked branches were almost muscular in appearance. The glossy evergreen leaves of the hybrids are variable, but always toothed – as in the *unedo* parent – whereas the stems exhibit the same richly coloured bark as *A. andrachne*. The small, white, pitcher-shaped flowers appear in late autumn or early spring depending on which parent is favoured by the seedling. As generally seen in cultivation, *A.x andrachnoides* is a handsome evergreen for the larger garden or park where it is particularly impressive isolated in a lawn or bed. Not surprisingly, it thrives best in a warm, sunny position in a well-drained soil, acid or alkaline. It is normally increased by grafting onto seedlings of *A. unedo*.

Betula albo-sinensis

There can be few people that do not recognize the silver birch *Betula pendula*, its Latin name referring to the weeping (pendulous) extremities of its branches. It is a name particularly well suited to this common tree native to Britain but even more applicable, in the opinion of some, is the old name *B. alba*, referring to the white bark for which this graceful tree is even better known. It is one of several different white-barked birches distributed right across the northern hemisphere from North America east to Japan. There are, however, other birches whose bark is anything but white though this is not to say that they are any less ornamental. My favourite among these has to be *Betula albo-sinensis*, a Chinese birch first introduced to the west in 1901 by E. H. Wilson. He collected his seed in the province of Hubei but the trees now established in British gardens are from later collections made by Wilson and others in western Sichuan, Gansu and Shaanxi provinces where it grows in mixed conifer and broad leaved forests in the mountains.

The name *albo-sinensis*, meaning 'the Chinese version of *Betula alba*' (= *B. pendula*) is an unsuitable reference in some ways as the two species are quite distinct. *Betula albo-sinensis* is a hardy, relatively fast growing tree up to 27m (90ft) in the wild but 15 to 20m (50 to 65ft) at present in cultivation. Its leaves are characteristically narrow in relation to length, thin-textured and slender pointed, producing a relatively light and airy canopy. In its bark effect, it comes nearest to the Chinese Paper-bark Maple *Acer griseum* for it is thin and peeling (often in large sheets) and a

Betula albo-sinensis – *young tree with bark covered by a glaucous bloom. Abbotsbury Gardens, Dorset (April).*

Betula albo-sinensis – *beautiful,
peeling reddish-pink bark, especially
effective in winter. Branklyn, Perthshire
(March).*

rich warm, coppery-pink colour. The young bark is coated with a
striking glaucous bloom. The variety *septentrionalis* (meaning northern)
differs mainly in its slightly longer leaves.

In China, this tree is known as the Red Birch and its beautiful stems
can be seen shining on the forest margin from a considerable distance.
In 1986 I visited a nature reserve known as Juizhaigou in the mountains
of north-west Sichuan. It was a beautiful area of rivers, waterfalls and
lakes of an incredible turquoise blue. The forested slopes above, which
sheltered pandas and white eared pheasants were full of fine trees such
as spruce, fir, maples and limes. But the one tree which caught my eye
above all others was the Red Birch which favoured glades and similarly
open sites. Its coloured stems, especially when bathed in the late
afternoon sun, seemed to soak up the warmth so that they glowed. One
ancient hoary giant we spied in a deep gully must have topped 27.4m

(90ft), at least, with a clear stem for almost half its height. The bark of the stem was dark, greyish-brown and shaggy, the coppery-pink younger bark confined to the upper branches. Like most other birches, *B. albo-sinensis* and its variety will grow in most soils only asking for an open situation away from shade. Its leaves turn a lovely yellow in autumn before falling and at this time, in my opinion, it is at its most impressive.

Being wind pollinated, many birches tend to be 'promiscuous' in cultivation, especially in collections where several species are grown together. This means that seed collected from any one tree is likely to produce at least a proportion of hybrid seedlings. Accordingly, nurserymen tend to graft *B. albo-sinensis* and var. *septentrionalis*, taking propagation material from correctly named trees to ensure that customers get exactly what they ask for. Where seed is available from birch in the wild the resultant seedlings can generally be relied upon to come true.

Carpinus cordata

The hornbeams are one of the most neglected groups of deciduous trees in cultivation. Apart from the Common Hornbeam, *Carpinus betulus* and its cultivar 'Pyramidalis', they are rarely seen outside of botanic gardens and specialist collections. With the exception of a few species from the warmer regions of the Himalaya and China, they are quite

Carpinus cordata – *young specimen showing rich autumn foliage. The Hillier Arboretum, Hampshire (October).*

hardy and easy, growing well in most soils except those which are badly drained or waterlogged. Although they have little ornamentally to offer in flower, there are several which, given the space, I would happily accommodate in my garden, solely for habit and leaf.

One of these would certainly be *Carpinus cordata*, a native of southeast Siberia, China, Korea and Japan, first introduced to Britain from the latter country by the Veitch Nursery collector Charles Maries in 1879. The name *cordata* refers to the characteristic, deeply heart-shaped (cordate) base to the leaf. It is a small tree of slow growth in western cultivation, reaching 8m (25ft) or more but apparently capable of twice this size in the wild. Mature specimens develop a rough, furrowed, later scaly, grey and brown bark, often commented upon by those who have seen this tree in the wild.

Young specimens in cultivation have numerous densely packed erect or ascending branches creating an ovoid crown but as the tree matures, the crown becomes more open and rounded or even tabular in habit. The leaves are relatively large from 6.5cm ($2\frac{1}{2}$in) to as much as 13.5cm (5in), taper-pointed, unevenly toothed and boldly parallel veined. According to one authority, this tree in America shows no propensity to autumn colour which is not my experience in Britain. For many years, a specimen in the Hillier Arboretum in Hampshire regularly, each autumn turned a rich gold. When I last saw this tree, it had attained a height of 8m (26ft) and an examination of its colourful canopy revealed the drooping, hop-like fruit clusters with their overlapping downy, pale brown scales.

Where seed is obtainable, *C. cordata* can be grown in quantity otherwise nurserymen have to resort to grafting this species onto stocks of the Common Hornbeam. Although it is never commonly available it is occasionally offered by specialist nurseries. Apart from the arboretum, *C. cordata* is worth considering as an isolated small tree in a lawn where its attractions can be appreciated from all sides. It is also worth bearing in mind for gardens or courtyards in city areas, so long as allowance is made for its eventual habit.

Cornus controversa 'Variegata'

There is a relatively small group of trees whose merits are considered so exceptional that the demand for them far exceeds their supply. One of these trees is *Cornus controversa* 'Variegata'. It is a variegated version of a tree found wild in the mountain forests of Japan, China and the eastern Himalaya. In these forests, *Cornus controversa*, sometimes called the Pagoda Dogwood, can make a tree of up to 20m (65ft) whilst in cultivation it averages 15m (55ft).

With the exception of the American *C. alternifolia*, *Cornus controversa* differs from all other dogwoods (*Cornus* species) in its leaves which are borne alternately along the shoots rather than in pairs. The new branches, which are an attractive dark reddish colour, are borne in uneven rings at the tip of the main shoot so that over a period of years, the tree develops a characteristic and highly ornamental tiered crown, an effect that can be enhanced by careful, selective pruning. The branches, with their slender, constantly dividing extremities, form wide fans so that a mature tree is often much wider than it is high. The small white flowers borne in flattened heads are not produced on young specimens but once flowering does commence the effect in summer can

Cornus controversa 'Variegata' – an old tree with characteristic tiered branching. Dunloe Castle Gardens, Co. Kerry (July).

be impressive, with the layers of branches appearing from a distance, to be coated with a creamy froth. The flowers are followed by small blue-black, berry-like fruits which are rarely numerous enough to be considered 'eye-catching' though they do make a nice contrast to the autumn leaves which sometimes colour purple or bronze red.

Imagine all the above qualities of habit and flower with the added bonus of a variegated leaf and *C. controversa* 'Variegata' takes a bow. First introduced from Japan by the English nursery firm of Veitch around 1890, this beautiful dogwood has become one of the most desirable of all trees. The leaves are much smaller than those of the green type and somewhat mis-shapen with an irregular, cream-coloured margin. This may not sound very encouraging but the result is both charming and effective. The poise of the leaves is such that they are evenly and elegantly displayed on the tiered branches, creating layers of light. This is particularly enhanced when the sun is shining and to stand beneath a mature tree in these conditions, gazing through the dark tracery of branches and pale chips of foliage at the blue sky above is breathtaking.

The finest specimen I knew of 'Variegata' grew in the garden of the Dunloe Castle Hotel, Killarney, Ireland. Unhappily, tragedy struck this tree in 1980 when it was killed by honey fungus. It had been planted in the early 1920s and was in the region of 10.5m (35ft) high and 12 to

13.7m (40 to 45ft) across when it died. Regrettably, 'Variegata' has proved impossible to propagate from cuttings and the only alternative, grafting, is painfully slow. Small quantities do find their way into the trade but most nurserymen offering this tree normally have more requests than they can satisfy.

Both *C. controversa* and 'Variegata' are hardy in all but the coldest areas and so long as waterlogged and very dry soils are avoided they are suitable for most sites, preferring shelter to wind. The name *controversa* meaning 'controversial' or 'doubtful' refers to the fact that this tree was originally known under the name *C. brachypoda* and on the continent as *C. macrophylla*, both of which proved to be incorrect.

Cornus controversa 'Variegata' – note the delicate tracery of the branchlets and leaves. Dunloe Castle Gardens, Co. Kerry (July)

Cornus kousa var. *chinensis*

Cornus kousa is one of the most satisfactory of all the so-called dogwood trees in general cultivation. More than that, it is one of the finest flowering trees for today's gardens. It is a native of China, Korea and Japan where it grows in woodlands in mountain areas. Indeed, its Japanese name 'kousa' was adopted as the scientific name of this tree by a botanist called Hance.

It is a small, usually multi-stemmed, tree up to 6m (20ft) on average,

Above: Cornus kousa *var.* chinensis
– exquisite star-like flowerheads. The
Hillier Arboretum, Hampshire (June).
Below: Cornus kousa *var.* chinensis *–*
young tree showing typical autumn
foliage. The Hillier Arboretum,
Hampshire (October).

though it will reach 9m (30ft) in a suitable situation. As a young tree it is relatively fast growing with a dense vase-shaped habit of growth. With maturity, however, growth slows and the branches develop a layered, fan-like arrangement not unlike that of *C. controversa* but never as clear cut. These branches have a dense cover of leaves which change in autumn from dark green to a rich medley of purple, orange and red. Indeed, its autumn effect is sometimes overlooked by writers understandably besotted with the brilliance of its floral display.

These flowers are curious structures. The true (functional) flowers are tiny and greenish and gathered together in a tight globular head. No one would give them a second glance if it was not for the creamy-white bracts which accompany each head. These are four in number, 5cm (2in) long and are arranged around the green head in a four-pointed star. They are at their peak in June but long before that they are attractive in their developing shades of green while much later they exhibit pink or rose tints as they age. In my experience, the variety *chinensis* has even larger flower heads so that a tree in full bloom gives the impression of a leafy fountain with star studded jets arching out in every direction.

After flowering, generally in a warm summer, the rounded fleshy fruits develop until by autumn, they are fully ripened to a dark red when they hang beneath the branches like large raspberries on slender stalks. A well fruited tree is almost as spectacular as a tree in flower, especially if, as is usually the case, they are accompanied by the smouldering autumn foliage. The fruits are irresistible to some people but while not poisonous their taste is insipid and the texture mealy and lumpy because of the numerous seeds.

As if all this change was not enough, old specimens develop an attractive mottled peeling bark on their main stems in which grey, dark and pale brown predominate. This is best appreciated in winter when the tiered arrangement of the leafless branches allows for better viewing. In addition to the variety *chinensis*, there has been a large number of selections raised in western cultivation including 'Milky Way', 'China Girl' and 'Summer Stars' all of which are claimed by their raisers to be improvements, though *chinensis* is hard to beat. There are also weeping forms and at least two variegated selections 'Gold Star' (leaves with a central yellow splash) and 'Milkboy' (leaves with an irregular creamy white margin). Some of the above are certainly finding their way into cultivation.

All forms of *C. kousa* are hardy and easily accommodated into all but the smallest gardens. Mature specimens go particularly well with buildings, their horizontal branching contrasting effectively with vertical lines. They are probably best used as single specimens in lawn, bed or border and make spectacular features on banks above water and in woodland glades. Although it will tolerate lime in the soil, it is undoubtedly at its best on well-drained, lime free soil in sun or partial shade. While *Cornus kousa* can be increased by seed, the variety *chinensis* and all selected or named forms are propagated by nurserymen from cuttings.

Davidia involucrata

Davidia involucrata – *the striking 'handkerchief flowers' of a mature tree. Hillier's West Hill Nursery, Winchester (May).*

Any tree that can take up to 20 years to produce its first flower must have powerful credentials if it is to become accepted by gardeners. Such a tree is *Davidia involucrata*, the Chinese Dove Tree. In cold areas it is often slow in growth while in the sapling stage its shoots may be damaged in severe winters. Otherwise, it is a hardy tree suitable for most soils but growing best on a moist deep loam, especially when sheltered by other trees as in a woodland glade or ravine. Some of the finest specimens in cultivation are around 20m (65ft) in height, often with large spreading, slightly conical crowns. Even taller specimens are known in some gardens.

At the other end of the scale is a tree growing in the Hillier Arboretum in Hampshire. It was planted as a sapling in 1964 and for 16 years I watched it increasing in size but with no hint of a flower. In 1980, I left the Arboretum and the following year the tree, then 7.6m (25ft) in height, produced its first flowers. In other situations and circumstances the Dove Tree has been known to flower in ten years or less.

The 'flowers' appear with the heart-shaped leaves in late spring, hanging below the branches. Essentially, each 'flower' is made up of numerous tiny petal-less male flowers with red stamens. These are gathered into a spherical 'brush' through which protrudes the green pistil of the single female flower. In itself this is not very ornamental but the absence of petals is more than compensated for by a pair of large, creamy-white leaf shaped bracts, one larger than the other. These hang either side of the flower head and flutter in the slightest wind, hence the

Davidia involucrata *var.*
vilmoriniana – *compact crown of*
young flowering tree. Kiftsgate Court,
Gloucestershire (June).

names Dove Tree and Pocket Handkerchief Tree. The name *involucrata*
refers to these two bracts which form an involucre, or protective sheath
around the flower head. The flowers remain fresh for up to two weeks
before falling to the ground leaving the young green fruits hanging
from the branches like baubles. Later, in autumn or winter, these too
fall, having by now ripened to brown with darker spots. Even in its
winter aspect the Dove Tree is worthy of note for the old bark is
orange and brown and scaly in effect.

The history of the tree is equally fascinating. It is named after a
French missionary and naturalist Armand David who first found it in
1865, in the then independent kingdom of Moupin, now part of
Sichuan, David sent dried samples of his find to Paris but it was not
until 1897 that another French missionary Paul Farges sent home seeds,
only one of which germinated. This seedling must have grown at

incredible speed for in 1906, at seven years of age, it flowered to astonish the gardening and botanical worlds. Farges' introduction, proved to be a variety of David's tree and was named var. *vilmoriniana*, after the French nursery firm of Vilmorin. It is this variety which is most commonly found in cultivation today and in colder countries it is said to be the hardier of the two.

Meanwhile in 1899, James Harry Veitch, having seen dried specimens of typical *Davidia involucrata* sent home from China by an Irish custom's official Augustine Henry, engaged E. H. Wilson to go to China with the object of finding the Dove Tree and obtaining its seed. After many travails Wilson was successful and it is thanks mainly to him that this outstanding tree is so well established in cultivation today.

Considering its eventual size, it is a tree that needs plenty of space although there is no reason why it cannot be underplanted with shrubs in a bed or border during its early years. Both *D. involucrata* and var. *vilmoriniana* are normally increased from seed which can take two years to germinate. Cuttings and layering are an alternative, but less popular method.

Embothrium coccineum

Well named the Chilean Fire Tree or Fire Bush, *Embothrium coccineum* has the most brilliantly coloured flowers of any hardy tree. They are a fiery crimson or orange-scarlet, narrow and tubular in shape and thickly crowd the branches in the summer. Indeed, when one sees a specimen in full bloom from a distance, it is easy to understand the relevance of its common name. It is native to the Andes of Chile and neighbouring Argentina as far south as the wild windswept 'Land of Fire' Tierra del Fuego. First collected as a dried specimen during Captain Cook's second voyage, it was not introduced as seed until 1846 when William Lobb collected it for the Veitch nursery of Exeter. Since then there have been numerous introductions which have successfully established this tree in cultivation.

In the wild, it occurs over a wide altitudinal range, from sea level to the upper limit of the forest where it is usually reduced by exposure to a dense low bush. One hears of mountain slopes dotted with hummocks of this tree in full flower, a spectacular sight. In more sheltered sites, it is larger and is commonly seen as a tree of 9m (30ft) or more. In cultivation in some of the milder, wetter gardens of western Britain and south-west Ireland, it has found conditions so much to its liking that trees sometimes grow to equal, if not exceed in size, those found in the wild.

Many, if not most, of the larger fire trees in milder areas of Britain and Ireland belong to a somewhat tender and evergreen form of the species quite unsuitable for colder areas. Far better suited to general cultivation are the forms of this species introduced by the plant collector Harold Comber in 1926–27 from a harsh and cold location. Unlike the older, less hardy introductions, Comber's trees are hardier and semi-deciduous with leaves variable in shape. One of the best of these is known as 'Norquinco Valley' from whence it was originally collected. Seedlings, and occasionally suckers, raised from this form are commonly available from nurserymen as are plants grown under the varietal name *lanceolatum*. This too, is generally hardier than the older, broader leaved introductions.

Above: Embothrium coccineum *var.* lanceolatum – *well named the Chilean fire tree. Crarae Gardens, Argyll (June).*

Below: Embothrium coccineum *var.* lanceolatum – *curiously shaped flowers in dense bunches. The Hillier Arboretum, Hampshire (June).*

To be at all successful with the Fire Tree, certain conditions need to be met. First of all it demands an acid soil, preferably one that is moist but well drained. Secondly, it does not care for wind or exposure, especially from the east, though it requires a sunny position if it is to flower well. Given these conditions and planted when small from a pot, there is no reason why a Fire Tree should not flourish. It is normally raised from seed when available otherwise from cuttings. It resents disturbance when once established but if conditions are suitable it will spread by suckers and seed to form a thicket of erect slender stems.

There is no doubting that it flourishes best in wetter areas where trees of 6 to 7.6m (20 to 25ft) are commonly seen in both private and public gardens. It also flowers from a relatively early age and specimens of 3 to 4.5m (10 to 15ft) are frequently heavy with blossom. One such tree in a pocket-handkerchief sized garden close to my home in Hampshire, annually attracts a great deal of interest and discussion from passers by.

The name *coccineum* refers to the scarlet colour of the flowers which are pollinated by humming birds in the wild. Also in the wild, there are yellow-flowered variants but these are extremely rare. At least one such form is rumoured to be in cultivation in Britain but enthusiasts may have to wait some considerable time before plants become available in the trade.

Eucalyptus niphophila

Of all the trees which grew in the Hillier Arboretum in Hampshire when I was Curator there, the Snow Gum *Eucalyptus niphophila*, was easily the most popular with visitors. There were (and still are) several specimens planted in different areas of the Arboretum, but one in particular was a special favourite because of its quaint leaning habit. Over many years the stem of this tree was stroked and hugged by innumerable youngsters who found the smooth marbled bark irresistible. There were occasions too, when adults found themselves likewise attracted and I well remember the day I introduced a group of the partially sighted to this tree. The smile on their faces as their fingers made contact with the bark would have made an Australian feel proud.

Most of the eucalypts – and there are over 400 of them – are native to Australia where they are found in a wide variety of habitats. Although they contain some of the most spectacular of all trees only comparatively few are considered hardy enough to plant in the colder areas of the cool temperate zones. These include the snow gums, a group of three or four species commonly represented in gardens by *E. niphophila* and *E. pauciflora*, the names meaning 'snow loving' and 'few-flowered' respectively. Two other species are *E. gregsoniana*, the Wolgan Snow Gum, and *E. debeuzevillei*. Although still rare in cultivation they are slowly being made available.

All the snow gums have several characteristics in common apart from their relative hardiness in our cool temperate climate. For a start, their adult leaves are comparatively large and lance, or scimitar, shaped, those of *E. niphophila* ending in a small curved or hooked point. As in all eucalypts, they are evergreen. The 'flowers' of eucalypts are petalless but more than make up for this deficit in their numerous coloured stamens which in the case of the snow gums are white. These flower heads are like fuzzy shaving brushes borne in dense rounded clusters

Opposite: Eucalyptus niphophila – *small exotic-looking evergreen with piebald bark. The Hillier Arboretum, Hampshire (May).*

along the shoots in summer. They develop from buds formed the previous year and collectively are rather spectacular and exotic looking.

Another characteristic of the snow gums is their relatively dwarf nature of up to 9m (30ft) on average, in cultivation, but commonly less than half this in the wild. Their main claim to fame however, lies in their beautiful smooth bark which when old peels away in large flakes and sheets, revealing the paler new bark beneath. At any time of the year, the main stems exhibit a most attractive mixture of grey, green and silver in various shades. The younger shoots of the snow gums are generally polished red or reddish purple but in *E. niphophila* these become covered with a white bloom adding considerably to their attraction.

As in all eucalypts, the snow gums are normally seed grown and are best planted young from pots into their permanent home during the summer. Older, taller specimens, especially if they are 'pot-bound', are not easily established and frequently fall over in a strong wind. Once established, they commonly form a low branched habit which may be changed if desired by careful pruning in the early years.

Coming from the alpine regions of south-east Australia and Tasmania, the snow gums are hardy in all but the coldest areas of Britain and North America although even in the warmer areas they can suffer in unusually severe winters, especially when wind chill factors lower the temperature. An established specimen of *E. niphophila* in my Hampshire garden had its foliage killed in the winter of 1986/87 but survived to sprout anew the following season. They are, however, fast growing and given a lime-free soil soon make a tree of character for the lawn or bed especially in smaller gardens where other eucalypts might grow too large.

Liquidambar formosana

In May 1979, I was in China for the first time visiting gardens, temples, factories and schools as joint leader of a Cultural Tour. In the playground of a school near Guangzhou (Canton), we watched a keep fit demonstration while sitting beneath three huge specimens of *Liquidambar formosana*, a Chinese version of the American Sweetgum *L. styraciflua*. They were old trees with massive stems and must have been at least 30m (100ft) tall. Later on in the tour, we saw this tree again, planted by the beautiful Lake at Hangzhou and wild in the hills above. I was struck by its seeming tolerance of adverse conditions while remaining healthy and handsome. In east China it is often planted by roads in cities and suburban areas where industrial pollution, compaction of the soil and bad pruning are common problems. In the western world, where it is rare outside of botanic gardens and specialist collections, it is a relatively uncommon tree and its merits are known only to a comparative few.

Liquidambar formosana is native to a wide area of central and southern China including Taiwan (Formosa) where it was first described and after which it is named. Trees from the more southerly areas of its range are not totally hardy in cool temperate zones, lacking the summer heat to which they are accustomed. Most of the trees found in the west are derived from seeds introduced from west China by the plant hunter E. H. Wilson in 1907. These are hardier and perfectly satisfactory in our conditions although unripened shoots are likely to be

Liquidambar formosana – *a young tree with leaves just beginning to colour in autumn. The Hillier Arboretum, Hampshire (November).*

damaged in cold winters. This introduction, once recognized as a distinct variety *monticola* (growing on mountains), is a handsome tree of medium vigour up to 12 or 15m (40 or 50ft). Its bold leaves are characteristically three-lobed, not unlike those of certain maples, but arranged alternately on the shoots. They emerge in spring a rich purple, paling to bronzy red and finally green. Before falling in autumn they again change colour from yellow to orange and crimson and are then at their most striking.

Given the space, *Liquidambar formosana* is a stately tree worth growing for its foliage alone. The flowers and fruits are of botanical interest only. It enjoys a sunny situation sheltered from exposure and preferably a lime free soil though I have known it to grow (but slowly) in a deep soil over chalk. It can be increased from seed when available but selected forms are normally grafted.

Magnolia campbellii

One of the most exciting late winter events in Cornwall is the flowering of *Magnolia campbellii*, a tree magnolia from the eastern Himalaya which has already reached heights of 20m (65ft) and above in western cultivation. Fine examples of this magnificent species are found in a number of the famous woodland gardens in Cornwall and each year, frosts permitting, the impulsive buds formed the previous summer burst from grey furry coats to expand their large, fleshy, pink or rose-coloured petals. The individual flowers resemble sumptuous waterlilies, poised on the leafless branchlets and in a good year a large tree at its peak can carry a thousand or more blooms.

The species was first discovered in Sikkim by Sir Joseph Hooker around the middle of the last century and he named it after his friend Dr. Archibald Campbell (1805–74), Political Resident in Darjeeling. In its native forests, *M. campbellii* commonly bears white flowers as pure as the snow on the peaks above. In cultivation this tree is known as forma *alba* and is occasionally available as a grafted plant from specialist nurseries. Some of the richer coloured forms of *M. campbellii* have been named and include 'Darjeeling' and 'Trewithen Dark Form' both of which are occasionally available as grafted plants from specialist nurserymen.

It is a relatively hardy magnolia. However, the susceptibility of its flowers to frost damage prevents it from becoming as widely established as it otherwise might. Another drawback concerns the time it takes to reach flowering maturity, 20–30 years from seed being not uncommon. Fortunately, those who long to grow this tree have the Scottish plant hunter George Forrest to thank for the introduction, in 1924, of a variety of *M. campbellii* known as *mollicomata*. Forrest's introduction, comprising several seed lots, was made in the mountains of China's Yunnan province, close to the frontier with Burma. Botanically, var. *mollicomata* is virtually identical to *M. campbelli* but it has the important horticultural merit of flowering in only half the time. Specimens of ten years (even less in optimum growing conditions) can be expected to produce at least a few blooms which are generally of a mauve-pink, rather than the rich rose-pink of the best forms of *M. campbellii*. There are however, forms of var. *mollicomata* which have richly coloured flowers and these are occasionally available as grafted plants from specialist nurserymen. The best of these forms is 'Lanarth' raised in the garden of that name in Cornwall, England.

M. campbellii and its forms appreciate a deep, lime-free loam which is moist but well drained. But for general cultivation, var. *mollicomata* is the most satisfactory of the two and not surprisingly it is the most widespread in western gardens. Even more suitable for general cultivation are a selection of hybrids between *M.* × *veitchii* (a *campbellii* hybrid) and *M. liliflora* raised by the late Dr. Todd Gresham in California. These include 'Heaven Scent', 'Peppermint Stick' and 'Royal Crown', all of which are free-growing trees with beautiful goblet-shaped flowers which are produced on quite young trees. 'Heaven Scent' is my favourite with its white flowers clouded rose purple on the outside. A seven-year-old tree in my garden is already 4m (13ft) high and has been

Magnolia campbellii – *over a thousand blooms are borne on a mature tree.*
Sharpitor, Devon (March).

Magnolia campbelli *var.*
mollicomata – *flowers like waterlilies*
on the naked branches. Knightshayes
Court, Devon (March).

flowering for the last four years. One of its strengths is the lateness of its blooms which rarely open until mid-spring when dangers of frost are receeding. In this character, it shows the influence of its *liliflora* parent. These magnolias are best planted in a site sheltered from cold winds, preferably by other trees. They can be grown from seed but the results, when they eventually flower, will be variable and in some cases disappointing. For guaranteed results, the best forms are grafted onto seedling stocks and although more expensive to buy are far more satisfactory in the long run.

Magnolia cylindrica

One of the finest young collections of magnolias in Britain is to be found in the Hillier Arboretum in Hampshire. Here, on soil which varies from an acid sand to an uncompromising clay, flourishes a wide range of wild species and garden hybrids, their flowers collectively beguiling visitors from early spring until the end of summer. The majority flower in spring and at this time, the Arboretum is a marvellous place to be, with magnolias and camellias on every side and the songs of newly arrived warblers among the awakening buds of the deciduous trees.

During my years as Curator of the Arboretum, one magnolia in particular always impressed me by its attractive vase-shaped habit and the poise of its flowers. This was *M. cylindrica*, a species native of Anwhei and possibly Fukien provinces in eastern China. According to the late Sir Harold Hillier, scions (grafting material) of this tree had been received by the Hillier Nurseries from the garden of the late Mrs. J. Norman Henry of Gladwyne, Pennsylvania in about 1950. Her tree had been raised from seed distributed by the Lu Shan Botanic Garden in China's Jiangxi province in 1936.

Since Hillier's began distributing *M. cylindrica* in the 1950s, doubts have been expressed among experts about its identity and some have gone so far as to say that the Hillier plants may even be a hybrid. Whatever its true status, there can be no doubting its ornamental merit and 'class' and as this plant is the one most commonly grown under the name *M. cylindrica*, it is the one I shall describe here.

In cultivation it has formed a widespreading bushy tree with often multiple stems and nearly horizontal branches. Some specimens are already 6m (20ft) or more, while a specimen in Cornwall, England, planted as a young grafted plant in 1959 had, by 1970 reached a little over 4m (13ft) with a spread of 3m (10ft). With careful pruning in the early years *M. cylindrica* can be encouraged to form a small tree when it may eventually come to exceed the height normally expected of it.

Long before the flowers appear in spring, the cigar-shaped buds are enclosed in an attractive rich brown furry casing. Gradually, these begin to open and the flowers emerge, cylindrical and erect. The name *cylindrica*, by the way, refers to the young fruits rather than the flower buds. Eventually the flower opens and for a time it retains a classic

Magnolia cylindrica. *Left: free-flowering nature of a young specimen. The Hillier Arboretum, Hampshire (April). Above: erect flowers of elegant form. The Hillier Arboretum, Hampshire (April).*

shape, narrow at the base, flaring out in the upper half. In colour it is creamy white with a pink stain towards the base of each 'petal'. Later, the petals spread widely when the flower assumes the shape of a waterlily. Of all the spring flowering white magnolias this to me is the most beautiful and elegant in flower. Once it has reached flowering size (only a few years on grafted plants), it flowers profusely and an established plant in spring, its flowers poised like candles on the leafless branches, is an experience not easily forgotten.

M. cylindrica is a hardy tree suitable for a lawn or woodland glade where its beauty can be fully appreciated. Like most magnolias, it appreciates shelter from cold winds and a lime-free, moist but well drained soil. It is increased by nurserymen from cuttings or grafting.

Magnolia '*Wada's Memory*' – erect in habit when young and very free flowering. The Hillier Arboretum, Hampshire (April).

Magnolia 'Wada's Memory'

I first met Mr. Ken Wada, a Japanese nurseryman, in the 1960s when he visited the Hillier Arboretum. I was given the opportunity of showing him round the collections and a pleasant and rewarding exercise it turned out to be, for his knowledge of plants, especially those of Japanese origin, I found prodigious. Over many years, his nursery exported great numbers of plants to the west and Hillier's had their share of his 'special selections', the results of his sharp eyes. The magnolia which bears his name, however, was one plant he gave away apparently without knowing it.

Sometime in the early 1940s, a batch of seedlings sent to America by Mr. Wada as *Mognolia kobus* were growing in the nursery of the University of Washington Arboretum in Seattle. One of the seedlings was considered to be sufficiently distinct from the others and to be worthy of special attention. Once this plant began to flower, suspicions were confirmed and it was named 'Wada's Memory' in honour of its originator, an unusual title to be given during the lifetime of the originator. It does, however, provide us with a striking reminder of a remarkable nurseryman.

It is a free growing, often multi-stemmed tree of conical habit, developing a more open crown in later life. With careful pruning in the early years, it is possible to encourage a single stem and a taller tree as a consequence. It is capable, eventually, of reaching 9m (30ft) or more and is spectacular in spring when flourishing its white, multi-'petalled', inclined or nodding flowers. These are much larger than those of *M. kobus* or even *M. salicifolia* to which species some experts now claim this magnolia belongs. The flowers too, are deliciously fragrant and produced even on young plants which is a valuable characteristic in an ornamental tree.

Given its eventual size, it is not perhaps suitable for the small garden though its relatively compact upright habit of branching as a young tree is more easily accommodated in a confined area. Like *M. salicifolia*, it prefers a moist, but well-drained, lime-free soil and shelter from cold winds. The leaves are narrowly oval to broadly lance-shaped and pointed, reddish in colour when young. It is normally increased by cuttings and combines most effectively when in flower with camellias. Indeed, a fine specimen in the Hillier Arboretum is associated with a bold planting of *Camellia × williamsii* 'Donation', the white of the former contrasting beautifully with the pink of the camellia.

Malus transitoria – *prettily lobed leaves in autumn. Talbot Manor, Norfolk (November).*

Above: Malus transitoria – the characteristic pea-sized yellow fruits, Talbot Manor, Norfolk (November).

Malus transitoria

Of all the many lovely ornamental crabs in cultivation, *Malus transitoria* is without question my favourite. I use the name with some trepidation as different authorities seem to have their own ideas as to what this crab really is. Some authors have described the crab under this name as being closely related and similar to *M. toringoides*. I would disagree. Having seen the last named in the wild in west China I can honestly say that it is quite different to the crab I know in cultivation as *M. transitoria*. To my knowledge, this tree has been grown by Hillier's for 30 years and may well date to William Purdom's original introduction from north-west China in 1911. Other nurserymen, in Britain certainly now grow *M. transitoria*, too, which is propagated by budding or grafting.

It can be grown as a large spreading bush but is normally offered by nurserymen on a single stem so that the dense rounded crown is carried well above the ground and is therefore more easily seen in a mixed planting. The tallest tree I have seen of this crab was 6m (20ft) and at least as much across. The crown is a mass of slender arching stems along which are poised small, neat, glossy green leaves most of which are distinctly 3 to 5 lobed and toothed, not unlike those of the common hawthorn (*Crataegus monogyna*) in shape. Before falling in autumn, the leaves turn a rich gold often with pink and russet tints. When they eventually fall, they create a splendid carpet beneath the tree.

The white flowers opening in late spring are pink tinged in bud and borne in clusters from short spurs all along the branches. These are replaced by pea-sized fruits which by the time the leaves are colouring in autumn, have ripened to a rich yellow. They continue on the branches into early winter or until eaten by birds. Considering its many ornamental attributes, it is mystifying why *M. transitoria* (if indeed this is what it is) has not been planted more widely. Like most of its clan, it is quite hardy and easy on almost any soil, acid or alkaline, flowering best in full sun. It makes an ideal lawn specimen except in pocket-handkerchief sized gardens and is equally suitable planted in a bed or border underplanted with low shrubs or ground cover.

Myrtus luma

Myrtus luma – *the lovely piebald stems of an old tree. Dunloe Castle Gardens, Co. Kerry (August).*

Some 15 years ago, I accompanied the late Sir Harold Hillier on a private tour of Cornish gardens. One of these, Lanarth, we reached by crossing Goonhilly Downs on the Lizard Peninsula. Once inside, we were soon engrossed in the rich, though sadly neglected, plantings once so lovingly cared for by the previous owner, the late Mr. P. D. Williams, and we found much to interest us, including many plants of Chinese origin. The most spectacular find was an old established grove of a South American myrtle *Myrtus luma*, an evergreen tree with small dark green, leathery leaves. The most extraordinary feature of this tree, however, is its beautiful piebald bark which is a rich cinnamon brown when mature, later flaking away to reveal a cream-coloured, sometimes pink-tinted young bark. The surface of the old bark has a loose granular surface which comes away on the hand when rubbed.

Seeing this tree for the first time stopped me in my tracks. The path we were following wound its way through the grove so that the stems stood on each side like the pillars of some fantastic palace. I have seen *Myrtus luma* on many occasions since but never have I experienced the same feeling as I had that day at Lanarth.

It is a native of Chile and Argentina where it grows in the forests of the temperate zones but sadly, it is not hardy in Britain except in the milder, wetter areas of the south and west. In many gardens and woodlands in these areas it has become so much at home that it seeds around, the seedlings often forming dense thickets. Here, too, it often reaches a good size, trees of 9 to 12m (30 to 40ft) being common. The largest specimen I have ever seen is a tree in the woodland garden at Glanleam on Valentia Island, Co. Kerry. When I last saw this tree in October 1981, I estimated it to be between 18 and 19m (60 and 65ft). The lower stems of this giant were filled with the scandent tumbling blossom strung stems of *Fuchsia* 'Corallina'.

In the same garden that day, I also saw a variegated form of the tree – *M. luma* 'Glanleam Gold', its leaves having an irregular, cream coloured margin. As the cultivar name suggests, it arose as a chance seedling and in 1981 was approximately 6m (20ft) in height. When grown in an open situation, *Myrtus luma* is generally stockier in habit with stout single or multiple stems and a dense compact crown. The darkness of the canopy is relieved in late summer and early autumn by a myriad of small white flowers, each with a central boss of stamens. A tree in full flower is a source of great activity attracting bees and other insects in search of nectar. The small black, fleshy fruits are both edible and sweet while the wood, as I can readily testify, is dense and heavy, not unlike that of the common box (*Buxus sempervirens*). In its native lands it is used for a number of household items including a Chilean version of the kitchen rolling pin, used to belabour errant husbands!

For those fortunate enough to be living in a mild area, *Myrtus luma* is almost a must, even if one does risk it becoming a weed. Although tolerant of lime (I have seen seedlings growing in crumbling cement walls) it undoubtedly flourishes best in a neutral or acid soil be it moist or dry. Apart from the obvious seed, it can also be propagated from cuttings. The name *luma* by the way is the Chilean name for this tree.

Nyssa sinensis

For many years during the 1960s and 1970s, I used to join the annual autumn pilgrimage to the National Trust garden Sheffield Park in Sussex to see the North American Tupelo *Nyssa sylvatica*. It was planted there in great numbers during the early part of this century and these trees are now handsome, dome-shaped specimens of impressive size. Indeed, one example recently measured was found to be 25m (82ft) in height. Attractive enough in its rich green, often glossy, summer foliage, the Tupelo excels in autumn when the leaves exhibit rich tints of yellow and red. Seedlings, of course, vary in this respect but given suitable conditions one can expect most of them to give at least some colour before falling.

Although commonly found in swamps and on poorly drained soils in its native climes, the Tupelo in cultivation will tolerate much drier conditions especially on acid soils. It has been grown in British gardens

Nyssa sinensis – *a young tree showing its brilliant autumn foliage. The Hillier Arboretum, Hampshire (November).*

since its first introduction in the early half of the 18th century, though it was by no means common until the present century. A century ago, in the wooded mountains above the Yangtze Gorges in China's Hubei province an Irishman, Augustine Henry, discovered a new species of Tupelo which was named *N. sinensis*. Four years later, following Henry's directions it was re-located by E. H. Wilson who then collected its seed.

Only one plant was raised from this seed but a few years later Wilson introduced another batch, this time for the Arnold Arboretum, Massachusetts, USA. For some reason, having been introduced, this species was not widely distributed and in Britain, at least, was virtually unheard of until comparatively recent times when Hillier's received grafting material from the Henry Foundation, Gladwyne, Pennsylvania. During the last 30 years, this exciting species has gradually become established in the major gardens and arboreta and is now available, though in limited numbers, from several specialist nurserymen who graft it onto stocks of the American Tupelo.

Having reigned supreme in our gardens for so long, *N. sylvatica* now has a strong challenger for our attentions in this Chinese newcomer. So far in cultivation, in Britain certainly, it has made a tree of loosely conical habit with ascending branches up to 6m (20ft) in height and there is every reason to believe that it will eventually achieve the height of 15m (50ft) given for it in the wild. From the beginning, the leaves of *N. sinensis* set out to attract us. The emerging leaves from spring, right through the summer months are purple, the colour slowly fading to green as the leaves mature. The fully grown leaves can be as much as 15cm (6in) long on a young vigorous specimen and if it had nothing else to offer *Nyssa sinensis* would be worth growing for its foliage alone.

Come autumn, however, the leaves begin to change in colour to yellow and orange, then a fiery red when the whole tree appears to have burst into flame. It is, in my opinion a superb tree for autumn colour, ranking with the best. It appears to be more vigorous than its American cousin and with a better habit. It is certainly as hardy, though I suspect that in areas with little summer sun, unripened shoots might be subject to damage in severe winters. All specimens I have seen so far have been growing on acid, sometimes sandy soils. Given its eventual size, I believe it should be treated as a specimen tree on a large lawn or in a bed or border, preferably sheltered from cold winds. The names *sylvatica* and *sinensis* mean 'of the woods' and 'of China' respectively.

Sassafras albidum

It is curious how the weeds of one country can be the treasured ornamentals of another. North America has many plants which are so common in places that they are ignored if not despised by those who live with them and cold shouldered by gardeners and garden planners. Sometimes, there is a good reason to avoid a plant, as in the case of the handsome foliaged *Rhus vernix*, the Poison Sumach, but in other cases the reason is probably one of familiarity.

The Common Sassafras, *Sassafras albidum*, is a native of the eastern and central USA where it is widespread on the moist, though well-drained, soils of open woodlands. In the south-east of its range it is one of the first trees to invade abandoned fields, forming clumps and groves by means of underground stems. As a result, it is not a commonly

Sassafras albidum – *the curiously shaped leaves in autumn. The Hillier Arboretum, Hampshire (November).*

planted tree in the average American garden though naturally it is well represented in botanic gardens, arboreta and collections featuring native trees. Even in Britain, despite it having first been introduced here in the 1630s, it is rare outside of botanic gardens and the like.

It is a hardy, deciduous tree of conical habit, eventually growing up to 27m (90ft) in the wild, but much less in cultivation.

Its winter aspect is distinctive with many irregular, flexuous, ascending branches, especially noticeable on young trees. The bark of the stem is dark reddish brown with deep furrows and ridges that eventually become corky, presenting a rugged appearance. The leaves are thin in texture, up to 15cm (6in) in length and variable in shape. Indeed, they are probably the most noticeable characteristic of this tree. A good proportion have either two or three while the remainder bear no lobes at all. They are always an object of curiosity, especially with children who liken the shape of the two-lobed leaves to that of a mitten or a boxing glove. In colour, they are a bright green above and bluish-green beneath, hence the name *albidum* meaning 'whitish'. In autumn, before falling, the leaves turn a beautiful lemon yellow or even orange to scarlet or purple, at which time the sassafras is at its most ornamental and eye-catching.

The tiny male and female flowers are borne on separate trees and are of no ornament while the fruits which are not always freely produced are small, dark blue and carried on scarlet stalks. All parts of the tree are pleasantly aromatic when bruised while from the bark of the roots, Oil of Sassafras is extracted for use in a wide range of domestic commodities. I remember once drinking Sassafras Tea, prepared from the roots of an English specimen by an American girl who later became curator of the National Herb Garden of America.

In cultivation, *Sassafras albidum* grows best in a rich, deep, lime free soil. It does not mind a moist site and will tolerate a dry situation without, however, attaining a great size. Naturally bushy when young, it should be encouraged to form a single stem by careful pruning. Any suckers that appear are best removed early unless there is space and the desire for a thicket. It prefers full sun so long as it is not in a cold, exposed site but is tolerant of shade. Although hardy it may be subject to some damage as a young tree during severe winters. Nurserymen normally increase sassafras by seed or root cuttings while suckers may also be moved with great care when small.

Sorbus cashmiriana

When I first moved to my present garden in 1982, one of my first projects was to make an island bed in the front lawn. I planted this with a selection of dwarf shrubs including slow growing conifers together with various spring flowering bulbs. In the middle of the bed I placed a multi-stemmed specimen of *Sorbus cashmiriana*, a native of Kashmir and a relative of the Rowan or Mountain Ash (*Sorbus aucuparia*).

Although it has bold, divided foliage which sometimes turns russet and gold before falling in the autumn, I have planted this tree mainly for its marble-sized fruits which are chartreuse green at first, gradually paling to pure white. From early autumn until Christmas they hang from the dark naked branches like bunches of precious pearls. If the winter is kind, they may sometimes be found still hanging, shunned by birds, into the New Year by which time they are invariably turning

Sorbus cashmiriana – *marble-sized fruits on red stalks. Author's garden, Hampshire (October).*

Sorbus cashmiriana – *pale-blush
flowers unusual for a sorbus. The
Hillier Arboretum, Hampshire (May).*

brown and decaying.

My specimen is sited where it can be seen from my study and ever since the first autumn crop of fruits, I have not for one minute regretted planting it. Fruits apart, *Sorbus cashmiriana* has another asset which places it apart from most others of its clan. The relatively large flowers are carried in dense clusters in the spring and instead of being white, as is the norm, are a delicate blush with a darker basal stain.

As a young tree, *S. cashmiriana* is firm and open in habit with stout erect branches and shoots, gradually widening as it matures to produce a broad conical crown, eventually reaching 6 to 9m (20 to 30ft) in height and spread. Like most other sorbus, it is hardy and easy in most soils especially those which are moist but well drained. It is not at its best on dry soils, especially during drought conditions. *S. cashmiriana* is said to come true from seed which is usually freely borne. It is also budded by nurserymen onto stocks of the Rowan.

Sorbus wardii

Over many years in the Hillier Arboretum, I grew to admire a whitebeam which flourished there virtually unknown, noticed only by the sharp eyed and the specialist. Its relative anonymity was mainly due to the wealth of other whitebeams growing in the arboretum, some with eye-catching bold foliage like *S. cuspidata*, the Himalayan White-beam and *S. thibetica* 'John Mitchell'. There were several specimens of this tree at the Arboretum, none of which had a name, only a number indicating that they had originally been grown from seed collected by the English plant hunter Frank Kingdon Ward in 1953 in the mountains between the two upper branches of the Irrawady River on the Burma–Tibet frontier.

Various experts on the subject have different ideas as to the correct name of this tree and I well remember a Russian botanist Dr. Eleonora Gabrielian visiting us on one occasion with the express purpose of seeing every sorbus we had. For the whole day we wandered around the 35 hectares (85 acres) of the Arboretum examining each tree in detail. When we came to the Kingdon Ward whitebeam, she suggested that it might be *Sorbus wardii*, named after the collector, which a Chinese botanist, the late Dr. Yu has since incorporated into another species – *S. thibetica*. For the purposes of this book however, I shall refer to it under the former name in view of its distinct habit, its history and its obvious garden merit.

As a young tree, *S. wardii* develops a characteristic columnar habit with close packed ascending branches. The tree broadens to form an ovoid column and in later life it spreads still further. Its leaves are broadly oval or rounded, and greyish green in colour at first, later turning green with greyish downy beneath. *S. wardii* leaves can be as much as 12.5cm (5in) long, but average 7.5 to 10cm (3 to 4in) and have a conspicuous ribbed appearance from the deeply impressed parallel veins.

The small white flowers in late spring are borne in few flowered clusters at the ends of short leafy branchlets and although of little ornamental merit in themselves are followed by clusters of substantial fruits which are yellow at first ripening to orange and finally brown. Of its kind, it is a first–class ornamental tree, ideally suited to an open site in a small garden or in restricted spaces elsewhere. It is quite hardy and amenable to most soils, acid or alkaline so long as wet conditions are avoided.

It has been propagated by budding onto stocks of the Common Whitebeam (*Sorbus aria*) or the Swedish Whitebeam (*Sorbus intermedia*) but it may well come true from seed. Supplies of this tree are maddeningly limited but once its merits are more widely recognized, its future availability should be assured.

Sorbus wardii – *russet yellow fruits and bold foliage. The Hillier Arboretum, Hampshire (November).*

45

Styrax hemsleyana

The Styrax, of which there are a good number native throughout the northern temperate regions, are generally regarded by plant connoisseurs as being among the most distinguished of ornamental trees for the garden. Quite why they should be regarded so is not easy to explain. They are free flowering when once established, but so are cherries and crabs. They are neither coarse nor untidy-looking trees, but neither are the majority of sorbus. They are not even large flowered like the magnolias (another aristocratic group). So what is it that makes them so special?

It is, I believe, a combination of all the above factors plus that almost indefinable quality; 'class'. They are certainly not trees to take the gardening world by storm. No local authority would risk using them to replace the countless 'Kanzan' cherries on suburban streets but they might consider trying one in a public park or garden should all other considerations be satisfactory. They are the typical connoisseur's tree, yet there is no reason why they should not be more widely grown in private gardens.

Probably the most commonly grown is *Styrax japonica* with its tiers of wide branches bearing showers of star-shaped, 'yellow beaked' flowers in late spring and early summer. Flowering at roughly the same time, but rather different in looks, is *S. hemsleyana* named after W. B. Hemsley (1843–1924), a Kew botanist and authority on Chinese plants. It is a native of woodlands in the mountains of central and western China from whence it was first introduced to England by E. H. ('Chinese') Wilson in 1900. Although hardy, it thrives best in a position

Styrax hemsleyana – a classic connoisseur's tree. Jenkyn Place, Hampshire (June).

sheltered from cold winds but open to the sun and away from the competition of other trees. Like most others of its clan, it prefers a deep, moist but well-drained, preferably lime free soil. Once established it develops a fairly compact crown of ascending branches gradually broadening as it matures. It reaches on average 6 to 9m (20 to 30ft) but in exceptional conditions can achieve more – the largest in Britain is a tree at Hollycombe in Sussex which had reached 14m (46ft) in 1973.

Its leaves are large, up to 14cm (5½in) long and 9cm (3½in) broad, few toothed and with a dark chocolate brown bud in the leaf axil. They often turn a clear yellow before falling in autumn. The flowers are at their best normally in June when so many other ornamental trees are competing for our attention and yet their poise and purity of white sets them apart from the rest. Individually, they are bell-shaped, five lobed, 2.5cm (1in) across and set in a small dusky calyx. They are carried in lax racemes or branching heads (panicles) from the tips of the shoots which bow slightly beneath the weight.

Very similar in effect is *S. obassia* which requires much the same conditions in cultivation. It is, if anything, a little slower growing but it develops a similar conical or rounded crown to 6m (20ft) on average but much larger eventually in optimum conditions. It differs also from *S. hemsleyana* in its even larger, more rounded leaves whose stalks, swollen at the base, conceal the buds.

The flowers are easily equal in beauty to *S. hemsleyana* and as a bonus are fragrant. A native of Japan and Korea as well as north-east China, *S. obassia* was originally introduced from Japan by the plant hunter Charles Maries in 1879. The name *obassia* is derived from the Japanese name for this tree. In recent years it has been introduced by a number of sources as seed from Japan and South Korea and fertile seed is the best means of increasing these trees, failing which they can be grafted or raised from cuttings.

Xanthoceras sorbifolium

Beyond the northern reaches of the Great Plain of north China is a vast area of mountains and deserts stretching into Mongolia. Once covered in forest, the lower slopes of these mountains are now relatively arid and clothed with a dense scrub in which thorny shrubs are dominant. There are yellow flowered roses (*Rosa xanthina*), junipers and pea flowered shrubs (*Caragana* species) in variety, thriving in the spartan conditions of long cold winters and long hot summers. Also found in this scrub and likewise shrubby, though it makes a small tree given shelter, is *Xanthoceras sorbifolium*, a member of a largely tropical and subtropical family that includes the sweet-fruited Litchi and Rambutan. It also includes another hardy relative in the Golden Rain Tree – *Koelreuteria paniculata*, likewise a native of north China.

Xanthoceras sorbifolium was introduced from this area by a famous French missionary Armand David who, in 1866, sent a seedling to Paris where it grew and flourished. It had, however, already been introduced to the Crimea in the early 19th century either by Russian traders or by missionaries returning from the Russian Ecclesiastical Mission in Beijing.

It is a deciduous shrub or small tree growing to 6m (20ft) in western cultivation with erect, pithy stems and spreading branches. The leaves are divided into numerous, narrow, sharply toothed leaflets like those

Xanthoceras sorbifolium – *a free-flowering old tree. Longstock Park Gardens, Hampshire (May).*

of a rowan or sorbus, hence the name *sorbifolium*, remaining green and shining until late in autumn. With the young leaves in late spring appear the flowers on the previous year's shoots borne in racemes 10 to 20cm (4 to 8in) long. Individually, they are 2.5 to 3cm (1 to 1¼in) across, comprising five crepe-like white spreading petals with a basal yellow stain which later changes to carmine. They give way to large, pendulous green fruits to 5cm (2in) across that split when ripe to reveal several dark brown seeds like small chestnuts.

It is from seed, when available, that this tree is normally grown though it can also be increased from cuttings. *Xanthoceras* does not demand a miniature Gobi Desert in order to thrive but given its native environment, it makes sense to plant it in the warmest, sunniest position in the garden. Some of the best specimens I have seen grew against south or west-facing walls and it is particularly suited to drier conditions. It is not demanding as to soil and will grow equally well on a chalky soil or an acid sand. It does not, however, care for heavy clay or ill drained soils. It is a rare and unusual subject, coarse in growth, elegant in leaf, beautiful in flower and curious in fruit. For plant enthusiasts with suitable conditions and the spirit of adventure, it is an irresistible combination.

Shrubs

Buddleja colvilei 'Kewensis'

'The handsomest of all Himalayan shrubs' is quite an accolade for a plant to receive especially when given by so great an authority as Joseph Hooker, later to become Sir Joseph and Director of the Royal Botanic Gardens, Kew. He was referring to a splendid buddleja he had brought back from his travels in the Sikkim Himalaya in 1849 and which he called *B. colvilei* after his friend Sir James Colvile. In the Himalaya this buddleja occurs from east Nepal to Arunachal Pradesh and is a member of the mountain scrub vegetation, especially on the edge of forest and where forest has been destroyed. Those whose experience with buddlejas has been limited to *B. davidii*, the Butterfly Bush and its cultivars, often find themselves perplexed when faced with *B. colvilei*. For a start it is a giant by comparison. A specimen on the chalk soil of a garden in Winchester, Hampshire was at least 6m (20ft) with a single stem when I last saw it some years ago and there are larger specimens elsewhere especially against sheltering house walls. In the wild it is reported to reach 9 to 12m (30 to 40ft), no doubt encouraged by competing trees and shrubs.

Even if the tree-like habit of this species does not unduly surprise one, the bold foliage often does. The long tapered leaves can be as much as 30cm (12in) long on strong, young shoots and are a dark green above and rusty, hairy beneath, at least when young. Add to its height and impressive foliage large funnel-shaped flowers which can be 2 to 2.5cm (¾ to 1in) long and as much across and one can begin to understand Hooker's admiration for this species and his undoubted excitement when he first discovered it. The flowers vary in colour from rose-pink to crimson and are white in the throat. They have a waxy shining appearance and in the early summer are borne from the ends of

the previous year's shoots in pendulous clusters up to 20cm (8in) long.

There are several named forms occasionally encountered in cultivation of which 'Kewensis' is perhaps the one most usually grown. Derived from a specimen which once grew in the Temperate House at Kew, it has somewhat narrower leaves than is normal and richly coloured flowers. It grew well in the chalk pit garden of the late Sir Frederick Stern at Highdown in Sussex and was regarded by him as the hardiest form although other more recent introductions of this plant from higher altitudes are likewise fairly hardy, though they may need winter protection when young. Otherwise they love sun and warmth and, except perhaps in milder areas and warm pockets, are best given the shelter of a south or west-facing wall. Like others of its clan, *B colvilei* is tolerant of most well-drained soils, acid or alkaline. It is increased by nurserymen from cuttings and is generally sold in containers.

Cistus populifolius

Few shrubs speak more of the Mediterranean sun and warmth than the rock roses or sun roses (*Cistus*). In one form or another, they are found in the wild over large areas of Southern Europe, North Africa and south-west Asia and are common constituents, together with rosemary, lavender and many other aromatic shrubs, of the low Maquis vegetation through which I have often picked my way on visits to the sunny

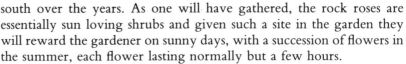

Cistus populifolius. *Above: ideal for sunny terraces and patios. Mount Stewart, N. Ireland (July). Below: flowers like those of a small wild rose. Mount Stewart, N. Ireland (July).*

south over the years. As one will have gathered, the rock roses are essentially sun loving shrubs and given such a site in the garden they will reward the gardener on sunny days, with a succession of flowers in the summer, each flower lasting normally but a few hours.

All are evergreen shrubs and mostly low growing, with flowers like small single roses, varying in colour from white to pink or purple. They are without scent but the foliage often makes amends for this with pleasant aromas. They grow best in a well-drained soil and are obviously more satisfactory in the warmer parts of the country, especially in coastal areas.

Some sun roses are undoubtedly more winter hardy than others and one of the hardiest in my experience is *Cistus populifolius*. It is a distinct and vigorous shrub capable of reaching 2m (6ft) in ideal conditions, but less than this on average. The handsome leaves, and it is worth growing for foliage alone, are heart-shaped, up to 9cm (3½in) long, attractively net-veined and a pleasant bright green. The 5cm (2in) wide flowers appear in early summer from the terminal leaf axils. The petals are white with a small yellow stain at their base which is further accentuated by the yellow stamens giving the flowers a yellow-eyed appearance. A variety *lasiocalyx* has even larger flowers.

The name *populifolius* meaning 'with leaves like those of a poplar' is not a very accurate reference though there is no questioning their distinction among all others. It is normally increased by nurserymen from cuttings and grown in containers. Young plants, curiously enough, are often more tolerant of lower temperatures than are old plants, especially those which have lost their dense compact habit. To some extent, this is true of all sun roses.

Clethra delavayi – *long, one-sided racemes held horizontally. Wakehurst Place, Sussex (August).*

Although they will grow on alkaline soils, the foliage of some sun roses, certainly, may eventually become chlorotic and they are best recommended for neutral or acid soils. They thrive on the acid Bagshot Sands of my garden in Hampshire. One of the finest specimens of *Cistus populifolius* I ever saw grew on the Dodo Terrace in the National Trust garden of Mount Stewart in Northern Ireland. It was growing in a south-facing border, a large mound of a shrub plastered with flower, its habit and foliage contrasting effectively with the stone of the walls and paving around.

Clethra delavayi

In 1981, whilst a member of the Sino–British Expedition to the Cangshan in Yunnan Province, south-west China, I saw *Clethra delavayi* in a dense thicket on the hillside above our camp. It was growing in an exotic hotch-potch of roses, hypericums, spiraeas, rhododendrons, mock orange and other shrubs and seemed very much at home with its 'head' in the sun and its flower spikes fully formed but held in tight bud. Just over a century earlier in these very mountains, this handsome shrub was discovered for the first time by the man whose name it bears, Jean Marie Delavay, a French missionary. Like so many of his persuasion, he was a remarkable man, full of enthusiasm and energy, an indefatigable traveller and a diligent collector of plants. During his years in China he discovered over 1,500 plants new to science, one of which was this clethra.

In the wild, it is capable of reaching tree size 9 to 12m (30 to 40ft) but is rarely over half this in cultivation. *C. delavayi* flowers in mid-summer and the cup shaped flowers 1.5cm (½in) wide are borne in dense, one-sided racemes disposed horizontally from the tips of the shoots. They are creamy white when open and when shed, leave behind the small calyx which matures to buff pink or rose. The racemes may be anything from 15 to 20cm (6 to 8in) long and a large bush in full bloom is a lovely sight. The dark green leaves are lance-shaped, 10 to 15cm (4 to 6in) long and attractive in their own right with their boldly impressed venation.

Unfortunately, *C. delavayi* is liable to damage in severe winters and except in milder areas it is best given the benefit of some shelter. It makes an ideal specimen for a bed or border especially in a woodland glade and is equally impressive when grown as a lawn specimen, but not in an exposed site. Like others of its kind, it requires a lime-free soil especially one that is moist but well drained. It is normally increased by nurserymen from cuttings.

Cornus alternifolia 'Argentea' – a characteristic tiered habit of growth. Cap Verde House, Jersey (October).

Cornus alternifolia 'Argentea'

For the many admirers of *Cornus controversa* 'Variegata' who reluctantly concede that their gardens are too small to do it justice, *Cornus alternifolia* 'Argentea' is an acceptable substitute. It is, in effect, a shrubby version of the other and one which is easily accommodated in the smaller garden. The habit of a young specimen is dense and twiggy and only with increased height do its branch tiers become more obvious. So slender and disparate are the branches, however, and so light and pleasant the leafage that its character can be enjoyed right from the word go.

The small leaves arranged alternately along the shoots, hence the name *alternifolia*, are pale green and irregularly variegated with white. They are so prettily disposed on the branches that they have the appearance of having been showered upon the bush like confetti.

The largest specimen I have seen was approximately 4.5m (15ft) tall by half as much – or slightly more – across, though it is undoubtedly capable of more. It produces small flattened heads of tiny, yellowish-white flowers in early summer which although of no special merit in themselves, serve to emphasize the bright leafage of the bush. Indeed, the name 'Argentea' meaning 'silver', well describes the effect. It is the ability to lighten dark areas which is this shrub's greatest asset, while the horizontal arrangement of its branches contrasts well with the sharp vertical lines of walls and buildings. It is a shrub which, as one American observer has written, 'stands out in a crowd', though this is not to say it should be crowded in a mixed border.

It looks superb as a specimen, especially in a lawn where it can develop unimpeded by neighbours. Add to all these qualities its hardiness and tolerance of most soils, acid or alkaline, and one can begin to understand why this shrub is increasingly in demand. It is increased by grafting or from cuttings.

Daphne bholua 'Gurkha'

On a cold, windswept Himalayan ridge one day in February 1962, an ex-Gurkha officer, Major Tom Spring-Smyth, collected three small

Daphne bholua 'Gurkha' – original seedling with Major Tom Spring-Smyth, Holly Cottage, Hampshire (January).

Below: Daphne bholua 'Gurkha' – sweetly scented flowers on naked shoots. Holly Cottage, Hampshire (January).

seedlings of *Daphne bholua* which he hoped might prove conducive to cultivation. The ridge was in East Nepal, not far from the Tibetan border, and several days march away from the nearest Nepalese road. Having carefully wrapped the roots of the seedlings in moist moss and placed them in a polythene bag, he packed them into a native porter's bamboo basket and sent him at a trot down the nearest valley. Eventually, the porter arrived at British Gurkha headquarters in Dharan where the seedlings were transferred to a jeep and driven to Calcutta. From there they were flown by the diplomatic bag to London to spend the next six months in quarantine at Kew Gardens.

On being given a clean bill of health, one seedling stayed at Kew while the remaining two were despatched to the home of the Major's parents in Hampshire. These were planted in the garden where they flourished for a time before one died, possibly from dryness at the roots caused by the too close proximity of a conifer hedge. The remaining plant grew to over 2m (6ft) and for many years, until its death from old age, flowered prodigiously each winter, beginning in some years shortly before Christmas and continuing sometimes into early March. This plant has been propagated and distributed under the name 'Gurkha', a reminder of these tough, hardy Nepalese mountain people.

Daphne bholua 'Gurkha' is a deciduous shrub with long, pointed, glossy green leaves and terminal clusters of tubular white flowers, purple-stained on the outside and deliciously scented. It is but one representative in cultivation of a species common in the mountains of the Eastern Himalaya. There, *Daphne bholua* (*bholua* being derived from the native name for this shrub) grows in woods and clearings, often suckering to form clumps, some individuals reaching heights of 3m (9ft), or more. The stems are flexible and the inner bark is used locally in the manufacture of a crude paper.

In the lower regions of its distribution it is evergreen and these forms are less winter hardy in cultivation. Those deciduous forms from higher altitudes have been referred to the variety *glacialis*. None of the forms can claim to be completely hardy except in warmer areas and even here severe winters can cause damage, if not death. A woodland site or a sheltering wall offer the best chances of success out of doors but even here frost and persistent cold winds can despatch the open flowers. Despite this, *Daphne bholua* is worth attempting in all but the coldest areas. Its fragrant flowers are a joy in the dull days of winter when there are few other plants to bring cheer. Their long-lasting qualities are a bonus, too. In the wild this shrub differs in flower colour and some very dark rose or rose-red forms have been reported in recent years, though they have yet to appear in the trade.

In addition to 'Gurkha', and a more tender evergreen form named 'Sheopuri', there is a splendid seedling of 'Gurkha' raised by a Hillier propagator and named after his wife – 'Jacqueline Postill'. I have a specimen of this cultivar by my front door where it has already reached 2.5m (8ft) after five years and increases its flowering performance each year. Apart from its exceptional vigour, its flowers are larger than those of its parent and continue over a longer period. If it has a weakness, it is the evergreen leaves which detract a little from the flowers.

D. bholua appreciates a moist, but well drained, lime-free soil in sun or partial shade. A specimen I once planted in a chalk soil grew and flowered well enough but its leaves become chlorotic and unsightly. It is sometimes available seed grown from specialist nurseries but the named forms are grafted and it is these that one should aim for.

Decaisnea fargesii

'Once seen never forgotten' is a comment often made about the fruits of *Decaisnea fargesii*, a deciduous shrub from western China. Its name commemorates both Joseph Decaisne (1807–82), one time Director of the Jardin des Plantes in Paris, and the Abbé Farges, French missionary and plant collector who first discovered this shrub in 1895 and introduced its seed to western cultivation. The fruits in question remind one in shape and size of plump pods of broad beans with rough skins, but instead of arising in erect clusters from the leaf axils, they hang in loose bunches from the ends of arching stems. It is their extraordinary colour, however, that sets them apart. This is a leaden blue without gloss, darkening with maturity.

The fruits derive from yellowish-green flowers of arguable ornamental value which are carried in large, loose, drooping heads below the leaves. The leaves, perhaps, are this shrub's second claim to fame. Shaped like those of an ash, they can grow from 60cm to 1m (2 to 3ft) long and a vigorous stem crowned with its bold foliage in summer is an impressive sight.

Although hardy enough, *Decaisnea fargesii* occasionally suffers frost damage to the young growths in spring but rarely does this seriously effect its subsequent growth. It is a loose-habited shrub with long erect or acending stems, 4 to 5m (13 to 16ft) – or more – tall, which become

wide-spreading with age. It will grow in most acid or alkaline soils but is especially appreciative of a rich loam to aid maximum development and foliage size.

While lone individuals will fruit at maturity, the most reliable and spectacular results are obtained where two or more plants are grown in close proximity. In one garden I know at least two large island beds have been given over to groups of this shrub. On a visit there one November I found these groups virtually leafless and heavy with fruit. What few leaves remained had turned a rich yellow.

In the wild, *D. fargesii* grows in thickets of shrubs and scramblers on open hillsides, its leaf-crowned stems often thrust above its neighbours. It is increased by nurserymen from the black, disc-shaped seeds which fill the pod embedded in a whitish pulp.

Drimys winteri var. *andina*

In 1578, a Captain William Winter returned from Sir Francis Drake's round-the-world voyage, carrying with him among other souvenirs, a quantity of aromatic bark. The bark, which he had found useful in combatting scurvy as well as an alternative spice in his crew's meat rations, proved to be that of a tree growing in the Magellan Region of South America. Some 200 years later, specimens of the tree were collected during Captain Cook's second voyage and Winter's Bark as it had become known, was given the scientific name *Drimys winteri* in honour of its original discoverer.

It is widely distributed in Chile and slightly less so in west Argentina and Tierra del Fuego where it is said to make a tree up to 20m (65ft) in height. Trees approaching this size are to be found in cultivation in woodland gardens of south-west England and in Ireland, where it is acknowledged to be one of the most handsome and impressive of all evergreens. Trees and bushes of lesser stature are to be found in many other areas especially in the wetter west where they survive all but the severest winters in warm, sheltered sites often with the protection of a wall. Even when badly damaged, *Drimys winteri* is capable of sprouting anew from the base during the following summer.

Not surprisingly, over such a wide range of distribution in the wild,

Drimys winteri *var.* andina – *a useful evergreen of low habit. Knightshayes Court, Devon (November).*

Drimys winteri varies usually in habit, size of leaf and hardiness. The most distinct variety is *andina*, a dwarf shrub found in the upper reaches of the forest and on exposed ridges of the Andes and the coastal range. First introduced by the English botanist and plant collector, Harold Comber in 1926, this is proving a first rate dwarf evergreen for all but the coldest inland areas.

Apart from its habit, it has the added advantage of flowering when quite young. The flowers, like those of typical *D. winteri* are ivory white and fragrant, measuring 2.5 to 3cm (1 to $1\frac{1}{4}$in) across and are carried in loose clusters from the upper leaf axils in summer. It is without question a cheerful little evergreen, the fleshy leaves a dark green above and bluish green beneath. It is far broader than it is high, a plant from Comber's seed at Nymans in Sussex having achieved around 1.5×4m (5×13ft) in approximately 55 years.

Although tolerant of an alkaline soil, it prefers acid or neutral conditions, especially those which are moist but not waterlogged. It makes an unusual and effective companion to heathers in a bed or border or with other shrubs of similar stature. In the wild in Chile it is often found in the company of *Desfontainea spinosa*, *Berberis ilicifolia* and bamboo (*Chusquea* species) as an understorey beneath wind-pruned *Fitzroya cupressoides* and *Nothofagus betuloides*. Although seed is produced, nurserymen normally propagate *D. winteri* and var. *andina* from cuttings.

Elaeagnus angustifolia var. *caspica*

The majority of oleasters (*Elaeagnus* species) in British gardens are of the evergreen kind as exemplified by the hybrid *E.* × *ebbingei*, a popular hedging shrub, and the ubiquitous *E. pungens* 'Maculata' with its gold splashed leaves. Less often seen, outside of botanic gardens and specialist collections that is, are those oleasters with deciduous leaves whose qualities lie more in their small, but scented flowers and abundant berries. Although few in number compared with the evergreens, they are, nonetheless, ornamental enough to be considered for planting in larger gardens, either in an informal screen or groups or as single specimens in the lawn or in the less manicured areas.

There is one deciduous oleaster, however, whose merit ascends all others and this is the grey leaved *Elaeagnus angustifolia* which although native to western Asia has gone wild in many areas of southern Europe. It was first recorded in cultivation as long ago as the 16th century and although its value as a summer foliage shrub is appreciated by all who have seen it, it is still relatively uncommon in gardens, although it was once commonly grown in the American mid-west along the highway. One reason for its scarcity has to be its size. It is a large shrub or small tree of medium to fast growth, commonly reaching 3 to 4.5m (10 to 15ft) high and as much or more across. If given time and ideal conditions, it will reach twice this. It is not therefore, a shrub for the small garden although I once saw a specimen in a small plot which had been trained to a single stem so that most of its branches were carried above and beyond the boundary fence, fortunately to the delight of the neighbours.

Its numerous wide-spreading, shining brown branches are often spiny which can make it a difficult plant to handle should one need to prune it. Ideally it should be given a position with plenty of room for development so that over the years it will produce a bold mound of narrow grey foliage. Its leaves are generally lance-shaped or a little broader – up to 8cm (3in) long – and are covered beneath, like the young shoots, with shining silvery scales which are even more beautiful when seen through a hand lens or microscope. The upper surface is grey and scaly, too, at first, gradually turning to grey green.

On any day in early June the garden may be filled with the scent of its tiny flowers which are borne in the axils of the leaves on the young shoots. These too, are silvery scaly outside and yellow within. Even more effective in the silvery sheen of its foliage is the variety *caspica* which is less often seen in cultivation but is gradually becoming more available. As its name suggests, it hails from the Caspian Sea region where it grows in dry stony places in full sun. Essentially, its leaves are shorter – up to 5cm (2in) long – and pointed, covered above and, more comprehensively, below with minute silvery scales. Seen in sunlight, these produce a shimmering effect which makes the Willow-leaved Pear (*Pyrus salicifolia*) seem dull by comparison. In habit it is a tall, loose-habited shrub with wand-like branches but is quite amenable to being trained to a single stem. Its flowers are similar to those of the other and borne just as freely in early summer.

Not surprisingly, given their native conditions, *E. angustifolia* and var. *caspica* love the sun and should always be planted away from shade. Indeed, the warmer and sunnier the conditions, the brighter and more effective the foliage. They are not fussy as to soil, growing as freely on

Elaeagnus angustifolia *var.* caspica – *shining, silver foliage in summer. Jenkyn Place, Hampshire (June).*

acid sand as on shallow chalk soil. They look superb when planted near dark green or purple foliaged shrubs and are also worth considering as a specimen shrub or small tree for the large sunny courtyard where they revel in the reflected heat. Being salt tolerant, they are among the most satisfactory shrubs for coastal areas.

E. angustifolia can be grown from seed when available, otherwise like var. *caspica*, it is usually increased by nurserymen from cuttings.

Euphorbia mellifera

Any gardener having holidayed in the Canary Islands will be well aware of the wealth of exotic plants found in the gardens there. Those more interested in the native flora will have travelled into the mountains and what little forest remains, to see such curiosities of the vegetable kingdom as the Giant Bugloss – *Anchusa* species, Moon Dock – *Rumex lunaria* – and that climbing relative of the Butcher's Broom *Semele androgyna*. These are but three examples from a native flora filled with curious, rare and sadly endangered species, many of them found nowhere else in the world. One group, the spurges – *Euphorbia* species – contains a number of ornamental shrubs and herbs including *Eurphorbia mellifera*, a native both in the Canaries and in Madeira where, in some situations, it attains tree size, up to 15m (50ft).

In the Canaries it is found in laurel forests on Tenerife and is also found on La Palma where, however, it is extremely rare and close to

Euphorbia mellifera. *Above: young specimens have a pleasing mounded habit. Abbotsbury Gardens, Dorset (April). Right: curious honey-scented flowers. Abbotsbury Gardens, Dorset (April).*

extinction. Fortunately, for conservationists and gardeners, too, *Euphorbia mellifera* has long been established in cultivation although it is very much a plant for warm climates. It is seen at its best in those regions where mild moist conditions are conducive to its health and development. Elsewhere, it is worth trying wherever Mediterranean plants succeed, especially if a warm, sheltered site is available. Once established and happy with its lot, it tends to seed around and seedlings are liable to appear in all sorts of places.

The tallest specimens I have seen in cultivation were easily 4.5m (15ft) with branching woody stems virtually bare of leaves except for those gathered towards the ends of the branches. The real beauty of this plant however, occurs in its youth when it develops a large compact evergreen leafy mound of stems and branches towards the ends of which the long, narrow, rich green leaves with a pale midrib are carried in bold loose ruffs. In spring, these are surmounted by loose clusters of brown and green, honey-scented flowers which attract bees and other nectar loving, insects. The name *mellifera*, meaning honey-bearing, refers to these flowers.

E. mellifera is a magnificent plant when happy, contrasting particularly well with stone, brick and paving. Indeed, some of the most impressive specimens I have seen grew in island beds on sunny patios or at the base of a wall where they have been planted when small from a pot. So long as other conditions are met, it seems unfussed as to soil, growing equally well in acid or alkaline. Nurserymen increase it by means of seed, whose availability is subject to the mother plant surviving severe winters. Usually, a well established specimen will come away again from the base if cut back by frost while young plants should be given winter protection until they have developed a woody framework. As in all euphorbias, the milky white juice of *Euphorbia mellifera* is caustic and care should be taken when handling this plant to see that the juice is not transferred to the eyes or mouth.

Fothergilla gardenii

Dr. John Fothergill, after whom this group of shrubs is named, was a Yorkshire born medical man practising in London during the 18th century. He was also a keen botanist, gardener and patron and around his home, Upton House in West Ham, he established a sizeable botanical garden which he filled with plants from far flung places of the globe. He was particularly interested in North American plants which he received from John Bartrum and other early American collectors. Naturally, he had one of the most extensive collections of American plants in Britain and he must have been delighted when, in 1765, he received a new shrub from one of his correspondents, Dr. Alexander Garden of Charlestown, Virginia. It was later to be named *Fothergilla gardenii*, thereby honouring the collector and his patron.

This is one of my favourite dwarf deciduous shrubs although, for some obscure reason it is not as commonly grown as its merit deserves. Granted, it requires a lime-free soil and thrives best in an acid sandy loam but this should be no bar to its wider cultivation. It is perfectly hardy and grows no higher than 1m (3ft) so is easily accommodated in the smallest garden, and where no garden exists it is worth considering as a tub subject.

F. gardenii has two seasons of beauty the first of which is in late spring

Fothergilla gardenii – *autumn foliage of brilliant hues. Author's garden, Hampshire (October).*

when the short, densely-packed, flower spikes appear from the tips of the still naked branchlets. The individual flowers are minute and without petals but they make up for this with their honey-sweet fragrance and long white stamens, with yellow anthers. Prettily disposed over the bush, they resemble little shaving brushes or miniature bristling milky white busbies. The leaves which follow the flowers are small and slightly leathery in texture, up to 6cm (2½in) long or slightly more. They are green above, and grey or even blue-grey beneath and quietly see the summer through until autumn arrives. Then, as if ignited by a spark they begin to change colour, yellow, orange, purple and scarlet following in succession until the entire bush is alight. Often all four colours are present in the leaves at the same time. Few other shrubs that I know, colour as richly as this and where soil conditions are amenable it should be in every garden, keeping alive the memory of the gardening doctor and Garden, his friend.

It is generally increased by nurserymen from cuttings. Although in the wild in the south-east United States it is found around the margins of ponds or boggy depressions, it is not usually demanding of moist conditions in cultivation. Indeed, a plant in my garden has flourished for several years in the company of heaths and heathers on a dry sandy soil.

Hamamelis vernalis 'Sandra'

Most keen gardeners are familiar with the witch hazels (*Hamamelis* species), deciduous shrubs from North America and East Asia. Their curious and often fragrant spidery flowers crowding the naked branches are one of the most welcoming sights in the winter garden. Come hail, frost or snow, one can always rely on them to brighten the gloom. Most of the witch hazels in our gardens belong to the Chinese *H. mollis* and its hybrids with the Japanese *H. japonica*. All have relatively large flowers ranging from yellow to gold, copper and red

Hamamelis vernalis 'Sandra' – like a smouldering bonfire in autumn. The Hillier Arboretum, Hampshire (October).

and in time make substantial wide spreading shrubs, or even small trees.

On the gravelly, often inundated banks of streams in south-central USA grows another member of the clan, *H. vernalis*, known as the Ozark Witch Hazel after the Ozark Mountains where it is particularly common. It makes a large shrub with numerous ascending stems to 3m (10ft). Later, these often begin to sag producing a wide spreading clump. In certain situations, suckers are produced, forming substantial thickets. The pungently scented flowers, unlike those of the Asiatic witch hazels, are rather small (up to 1cm (½in) across), and although produced in large numbers do not attract one's attention in the same way as the others. They range in colour from yellow to bronze (or reddish) and, in the words of one American observer, 'create a warm haze' when seen from a distance. The flowers open early in the year, hence the name *vernalis* meaning 'of Spring' and because the petals roll up on very cold days they last for a considerable period.

H. vernalis was first introduced into Britain in about 1910 but faced with the larger flowered Asiatic witch hazels it has remained in relative obscurity. In recent years, however, this species has been drawing more attention to itself in the shape of a selection named 'Sandra'. This arose as a seedling in the now defunct Hillier Nursery at Chandlers Ford, Hampshire in 1962. In the spring of that year, Peter Dummer, one of Hillier's master propagators, was casting his eye over a batch of some 2,000 seedlings of *Hamamelis vernalis* when he spotted a splash of purple amidst the green. Making his way through the batch he picked out a single seedling whose young leaves were attractively suffused with plum purple. This was planted out in a nearby bed where it continued to produce young leaves of the same colour throughout the summer.

In the autumn, when the leaves of *H. vernalis* were turning butter yellow, those of the selected seedling produced a breathtaking display of colour in which orange, purple, flame and crimson fought for dominance. And so it has been ever since. The seedling was named 'Sandra' after Dummer's daughter and is gradually becoming more widely distributed in gardens though, as yet, only a few nurserymen are growing it. It grows with the same vigour as the common type and is ultimately capable of the same size. Propagation is normally done by grafting though with skill and care they can be increased from cuttings.

Another selection of *H. vernalis* worth considering, when available, is 'Lombart's Weeping', a Dutch raised seedling with lax or drooping branches. In time these make a wide mound of close packed leafy growth. 'Lombart's Weeping' excels in autumn when the leaves turn yellow and I shall never forget once seeing a group of three specimens planted on a bank above a path in the University of British Columbia Botanic Garden in Vancouver. From a distance they looked to be heaps of gold and when I came close I could see that the branches which formed the mound, continued along the ground to form an apron of growth like the brim of a hat.

Of all the witch hazels, *H. vernalis* is perhaps the most lime tolerant though it undoubtedly thrives best in an acid to neutral soil. It is a hardy shrub, certainly, and is fairly tolerant of shade although it colours best in full sun. Whilst it is tolerant of a moist situation, it is just as happy in an ordinary garden soil and will even grow in heavy clay soils. Because of its wide-spreading habit when mature, it is best given plenty of space and its tolerance of moist situations can be put to good use in planting stream banks or lakesides since it is an ideal companion for colour-stemmed dogwoods and willows.

Hebe hulkeana

The shrubby veronicas of New Zealand are represented in cultivation by a wide range of species and hybrids some of which are among the most free flowering and long flowering of all evergreen shrubs. It is only when one takes a close look at their flowers, and later their fruits, however, that their relationship to the speedwells (*Veronica* species) of the Northern Hemisphere can clearly be seen. Variable in both hardiness and in ornamental merit, there are few, if any, gardens that cannot accommodate at least one of their number. Of all the hebes I have grown, I regard *H. hulkeana* as being the most pleasing.

For a start, it is a dwarf shrub rarely more than 1m (3ft) high by as much or more across with erect and spreading stems and slender, purplish-red branches. The leathery, finely toothed leaves 2.5 to 5cm (1 to 2in) long are a bright glossy green above with a narrow reddish margin. Pretty enough in leaf, it really attracts one's attention in early summer when the flowers are produced in large terminal branched heads (panicles). Individually, they are small, less than 1cm (⅓in), but are produced in such large numbers as to form plumes of pale violet or lavender, hence the common name New Zealand Lilac. Unlike the average lilac, however, they are scentless.

The name *hulkeana* commemorates Mr. T. H. Hulke who is said to have first discovered this species. It is a native of the north-east corner of South Island where it is found on dry, rocky cliffs and bluffs from sea-level up to 900 m (3,000ft). Introduced to British cultivation around 1860, 20 years later it was the recipient of a First Class Certificate from the Royal Horticultural Society when exhibited as a

Hebe hulkeana – *well named New Zealand lilac though lacking in fragrance. Royal Botanic Gardens, Kew (May).*

greenhouse shrub. It continued to be regarded as a very tender shrub until comparatively recent times and now it is grown outside in many gardens in southern and western parts of Britain and in warmer areas elsewhere. These may well be derived from plants growing in the higher levels of its distribution which would be hardier than those originally collected at lower levels.

Hebe hulkeana will grow in most soils, acid or alkaline, so long as they are well drained. It loves full sun and in colder areas may be given the protection of a south or west-facing wall against which it will sometimes reach as much as 2m (6ft), especially when given a wire or trellis support. In my previous garden on the chalk downs above Winchester, I grew this lovely shrub in a south-west facing border where it flourished in a soil composed almost entirely of rubble. There is no doubt in my mind that it is longer lived and tougher in such conditions than in a deep, rich loam.

In some gardens it has been known to seed itself around, seedlings appearing in all manner of situations including the crevices of dry or crumbling walls. It is raised by nurserymen from cuttings and a spare young plant is well worth keeping in a cold frame or greenhouse over winter to replace any plants lost outside.

A related species from the Banks Peninsula in South Island where it grows in volcanic rock, is *H. lavaudiana*. It differs from *H. hulkeana* in its more dwarf habit, smaller leaves and denser, shorter heads of white or mauvish flowers. Equally impressive is *H.* 'Fairfieldii', considered to be a hybrid between *H. hulkeana* and *H. lavaudiana*. It is somewhat intermediate in height and leaf, differing from the former in its shorter, broader heads of lavender-violet flowers.

Another first rate hybrid for the small garden is *H.* 'Hagley Park', said to be a result of *H. hulkeana* crossing with *H. raoulii*. It is a dwarf shrub, rarely above 50cm (20in) with crowded heads (panicles) of rose-purple flowers, darker in bud. The seed heads of all the above are best removed immediately after flowering in order to help conserve energy. This can easily be achieved either with secateurs or shears.

Hydrangea quercifolia

The majority of hydrangeas seen in our gardens are Asiatic species, or hybrids derived from them. The tall stately *Hydrangea aspera* from the eastern Himalaya and China and the numerous Hortensia hydrangeas derived from a Japanese species are well enough known in cultivation but not so the North American hydrangeas. This is in part due to their small numbers (two species and two varieties) and to their white, rather than coloured flowers. The most distinct of the two is *Hydrangea quercifolia*, the name derived from *Quercus* (oak) and *folia* (leaf) – the Oak-leaved Hydrangea. The kind of oak the botanist who named this hydrangea had in mind was not the English oak, of course, but one of the North American Black oaks, *Q. rubra* possibly. It is native to the south-eastern United States in the states of Georgia, Florida, Alabama and Missouri and although it was first introduced to Britain in 1803, it is still relatively uncommon.

It is a suckering shrub with erect stems to 1.5m (5ft), taller in the wild, in time forming a fairly loose mound much broader than high. The leaves are unlikely to be confused with those of any other hydrangea, being boldly 3 to 7 lobed and 15 to 20cm (6 to 8in) long. They are dark

Hydrangea quercifolia – *bold foliage of characteristic shape. Bodnant Gardens, N. Wales (August).*

green and smooth above with a contrasting pale or whitish felted undersurface. It is worth growing for its foliage effect alone, especially in autumn when the leaves often exhibit rich tints before falling, though seedlings are variable in this respect.

The flowers are produced throughout the summer and often to early autumn in dense terminal, sometimes conical heads (panicles) 20 to 25cm (8 to 10in) long, occasionally more. They are composed mainly of tiny fertile, greenish-white flowers of no ornamental merit on the outside of which are sprinkled much larger, sterile, white florets 2.5 to 3.5cm (1 to 1½in) across. It is the sterile florets which make the flower-heads so attractive in the same way as those of *Hydrangea paniculata* from north east Asia. As they age, the florets turn a purplish-pink and then brown. Even better to some eyes are several American selections in which the majority of flowers are sterile and enlarged giving the flower head a denser, more spectacular appearance. Two of the best are 'Harmony' and 'Snow Queen' while in 'Snowflake', the florets have numerous sepals producing a beautiful double effect. All three tend to have larger heavy flower heads which weigh down the branches. Of these, only 'Snowflake' is as yet available in British cultivation and then only recently.

Although *H. quercifolia* is hardy in all but the coldest areas of the cool temperate zones, it generally does best where conditions are more consistently warm and moist. Young plants may have to be given winter protection in colder areas until a woody framework of stems has been developed. It does not care for dry soils nor drought, preferring a fertile, moist but well-drained soil in sun or partial shade. In poor soils, dense shade or in cold areas its flowering is too inconsistent for it to be considered a quality flowering shrub though its foliage is nearly always worthwhile. In gardens where it flourishes, it is a shrub of great character and ornament.

It is normally increased from seed or from cuttings, though layers and suckers can be re-established given care.

Indigofera heterantha

The indigoferas, of which there are many, are members of the pea family (*Leguminosae*) and mostly found in the wild in tropical and subtropical regions. Of the hardier species, several are grown though none commonly in western gardens. Most indigoferas are of Chinese origin but there are two species from the western end of the Himalaya which are cultivated here. The most frequently encountered and most ornamental is *Indigofera heterantha*, sometimes found under its better known, though invalid name, *I. gerardiana*. The latter name at least has the advantage of historical interest in that it commemorates Patrick Gerard (1795–1835), an army officer. He was one of three brothers, all military men serving in India and collecting plants on their Himalayan travels, most of which were sent to the famous Dr. Nathaniel Wallich, then Superintendent of the Calcutta Botanic Garden.

The correct name for this shrub – *heterantha* – is derived, however, from the Greek and means 'various' or 'diverse' flowered. It is a deciduous shrub with erect shoots up to 1m (3ft) high, twice as much or more against a wall. The shoots are clothed with small leaves which are divided – ash like – into numerous small leaflets. The small rosy-purple pea flowers are borne in slender, tapering clusters (racemes) 7.5 to 12.5cm (3 to 5in) long from the leaf axils in the upper third of the shoots. Opening from the bottom upwards, they provide colour throughout the summer. At its peak it is a most striking flowering shrub providing colour of an intensity and vibrance not often seen in our climate.

In the wild it is often found growing in dry poor soils, always in full sun. Indeed, a hot, sunny situation in a well-drained acid or alkaline soil is the only way to obtain full satisfaction from this shrub in the garden. In cold areas or in severe winters elsewhere, it is normally cut to ground level but sprouts anew each spring to form sheafs or thickets of long slender shoots. Fortunately, the flowers are borne on the current year's wood which ensures a regular crop to gladden the eye. In all but the

Indigofera heterantha. *Above: thriving against a sunny wall. Cambridge University Botanic Garden (June). Left: richly coloured pea-flowers. Cambridge University Botanic Garden (June).*

warmest areas it is probably best grown against a south or west wall where it can be trained fan-wise, by tying its shoots into a wire frame or wooden trellis.

It is increased by nurserymen from seed or cuttings.

Leycesteria crocothyrsos

Many gardners have seen, if not grown, the so-called Himalayan Honeysuckle – *Leycesteria formosa* with its purple bracted, white flowers and caramel flavoured edible berries. Few, however, have grown its more tender and rarely seen relative *L. crocothyrsos*. This is a free-growing shrub, to 2m (6ft) or more with the hollow young shoots typical of the group. They are produced in clumps and are clothed with pairs of rich green, slender pointed leaves up to 15cm (6in) long, sometimes more on strong growths. The rich yellow tubular flowers are borne in summer in dense, drooping, tapering heads (racemes) from the tips of the current year's shoots. It is a handsome shrub in leaf and flower but suitable only for the mildest areas where it grows best in a sunny sheltered position, especially against a warm wall.

It is tolerant of any well-drained soil, acid or alkaline and should it be cut to the ground in a severe winter will usually sprout again from below during the following spring or summer. The fruits are like soft gooseberries and are packed with tiny seeds which afford this shrub's best method of increase, otherwise it is grown from cuttings.

L. crocothyrsos was brought into cultivation from the Delei Valley, Assam by the plant hunter Frank Kingdon Ward in 1928. He later described finding but a single plant of this shrub growing from a 'terrifying cliff' down which he had descended by shaky ladders. The first time I saw it was at Hillier's West Hill Nursery in Winchester where it was grown in a cool greenhouse which received a little heat in winter. A plant from this stock was later established in the garden of Dunloe Castle Hotel, Killarney, County Kerry where it grows still despite having been raised to the ground by frost on a number of occasions. The name *crocothyrsos*, by the way, refers to its saffron coloured flower heads.

Magnolia liliflora 'Nigra'

When I first moved into my present garden, I found I had inherited four sizeable shrubs, a motley collection of small fruit trees and bushes plus an equally motley selection of coarse hedges. Nothing to get excited about I told myself except that three of the shrubs were old bushy magnolias some 2m (6ft) tall and wide. I had my suspicions about their identities but it was not until the following spring when they came into flower that I was to confirm that all three belonged to *Magnolia liliflora* 'Nigra'. For many years, I have counted this magnolia among my special favourites and I further regard it as being one of the loveliest and most reliable of its kind.

After the star magnolia – *M. stellata* – this is perhaps the most suitable for smaller gardens, though it is equally impressive when planted in a large lawn or border. It is capable eventually of reaching 4m (13ft) in height and as much or more across but is relatively slow growing and compact in habit with dark green, glossy-topped leaves. The flowers

Leycesteria crocothyrsos – *a free growing tender shrub for mild areas. Dunloe Castle Gardens, Co. Kerry (July).*

Opposite: Magnolia liliflora 'Nigra' – *one of the longest flowering of all magnolias. Jenkyn Place, Hampshire (May).*

are borne at the ends of short branchlets or spurs, beginning in mid-spring and opening in succession until early summer. They are narrowly vase-shaped at first with pointed petals to 12.5cm (5in) long, later opening wide like water lilies. In colour, they are a rich, vinous purple on the outside and white clouded purple on the inside, creating a pleasing bi-colour effect.

This magnolia is a distinct and easily-recognized form of the so-called lily flowered magnolia – *M. liliflora*, which was introduced into western cultivation from Japan as long ago as 1790, the first 'coloured' flowered magnolia to appear in European gardens. Although grown in Japan for many centuries, *M. liliflora* is only known in gardens there and is thought to have originated in the wild in central China, south of the Yangtze. 'Nigra' itself was introduced from Japanese cultivation in 1861 by John Gould Veitch, elder son of James Veitch founder of the famous Chelsea and Coombe Wood nurseries. According to modern authoritative opinion, the correct name for *M. liliflora* is *M. quinquepeta* (with six petals), but for the purposes of this book, the better known (and far more appropriate) name, is retained.

M. liliflora 'Nigra' is one of the longest flowering of all magnolias. Even if the first flush of dark erect cigar-shaped buds are destroyed by late frosts, as they sometimes are, there are so many undeveloped buds in reserve that within a week or two the branches are once again bedecked with flowers. These continue in succession well into early summer and often beyond. For the last three years I have found the odd flower on my specimens in late summer and sometimes there is a flush at this time. Admittedly, these later flowers are often smaller than those of the mainstream blooms in late spring but they are welcome nonetheless. The leaves, too, with their characteristic gloss are a perfect foil for the dark flowers as they expand to show their paler interior. In a normal year, the first flowers appear on the still naked branches but the new leaves are not far behind and by late May the branches are well clothed. Even young plants will produce flowers which is a bonus for those gardeners who for one reason or another, want early results from their investments.

Both *M. liliflora* and 'Nigra' thrive in a moist, but well-drained, lime-free soil preferably acid. But they are tolerant of heavier (clay) soils, too, so long as they are not waterlogged. They are hardy in all but the coldest areas of the cool temperate zones where, however, they often respond to the protection of a south or south-west facing wall.

In an attempt to produce later flowering, shrubby magnolias to avoid damage from late frosts, a series of hybrids was made at the United States National Arboretum in Washington between forms of *M. liliflora* and the Star magnolia *M. stellata*. The results, referred to by one American observer as 'The Little Girl Hybrids', because all bear girls' names, are now available from several British nurserymen too and are worth considering, especially for small gardens. They are multistemmed, erect or conical and rarely grow taller than 4m (13ft). Their flowers are often large and shaped like those of the *liliflora* parent while their colours are in various red or reddish-purple shades. Their names are 'Ann', 'Betty', 'Jane', 'Jody', 'Pinky', 'Randy', 'Ricki' and 'Susan'. All who have seen them have their particular favourite, mine is 'Susan' while 'Ann' with smaller flowers, is a close second. All these hybrids, plus *M. liliflora* and 'Nigra', are increased by nurserymen from cuttings.

Mahonia nervosa

Despite it having been introduced to Britain as long ago as 1822, *Mahonia nervosa* has never been widely grown in gardens here nor is it commonly found in nurserymen's catalogues though it is thankfully available from some specialist growers. Whilst it is not as tough and amenable in cultivation as the ubiquitous *M. aquifolium* and its hybrids, *M. nervosa* is just as hardy and ornamental and well worth persevering with in gardens where a free root run and a little summer shade can be provided. It is a low, evergreen shrub, spreading by means of suckers to form large colonies in time. Its short erect stems 30 to 40cm (12 to 16in)

Mahonia nervosa – *colourful evergreen ground-cover in winter. Knightshayes Court, Devon (November).*

tall, bear several large handsome leaves shaped like those of an ash and are up to 45cm (18in) long. The leaflets are firm and leathery in texture and edged with well-spaced, spiny teeth. Dark glossy green in summer, they often become suffused with red or purple in autumn at which time, and throughout winter, they look superb as an underplanting to deciduous trees such as sorbus and snake-bark maples.

The small yellow, cup-shaped flowers are crowded into bunches of erect finger-like racemes 15 to 20cm (6 to 8in) long in late spring. They are sometimes followed by rounded bluish-black berries with a greyish bloom. It is native to western North America, from British Columbia south to California where it is found in coniferous forests. Two years ago I saw it growing in the coastal redwood forest of California and later beneath the shade of Douglas fir and Big-leaf maple (*Acer macrophyllum*) in Washington State. In cultivation it enjoys a lime-free soil, moist, but well drained. Naturally it is tolerant of shade but is not suitable for dry shade such as is found beneath a dense low, evergreen canopy.

While hardy, *M. nervosa* is not suitable for cold exposed sites and is at its best in the shelter of trees or taller shrubs. It is increased by nurserymen from seed when available, rarely by cuttings, and with care, suckers may be detached and established from established clumps. The descriptive name *nervosa* refers to the conspicuous venation of the leaflets.

Ozothamnus rosmarinifolius

For mild areas of the British Isles and in warm pockets elsewhere the various species of *Ozothamnus* are among the most satisfactory of all evergreen shrubs grown for flower. They are native to Australia, including Tasmania, and are closely related to, and sometimes included in, *Helichrysum*, having terminal clusters of small flower-heads which are a mixture of tiny tubular flowers and papery bracts. *Ozothamnus rosmarinifolius* takes its name from the narrow green, needle-like leaves which are similar in form to those of the Common Rosemary (*Rosmarinus officinalis*). They are also covered in tiny warts and densely crowd the erect, white-woolly branches.

In its early years, given space, it will form a rounded or hummock-shaped bush, dense and compact, 1 to 1.2m (3 to 4ft) high and as much or more across. Eventually, especially when grown against a warm wall, it is capable of 2m (6ft). Older plants tend to lose the compact habit of youth and can become scrappy and unsightly. When this happens they are best removed and replaced by a young plant. Although the leaves are an attractive rich green in colour, this shrub is mostly grown for its flower heads in summer which are red in bud and quite striking over a period of two weeks or more before opening to white with red outer scales.

In the wild it grows on wet peaty heaths and along water-courses in New South Wales, Victoria and Tasmania but in cultivation it appears to appreciate a well-drained soil in full sun. Although it seems equally at home on acid or alkaline soils, some of the best specimens I have seen grow in the acid soils and moist but relatively warm gardens of County Kerry in Ireland. It makes an ideal courtyard subject especially in town gardens where the reflected warmth is very much to its liking and it also flourishes by the sea in warmer areas.

Ozothamnus rosmarinifolius. *Above: compact mounded habit of a young specimen. Dunloe Castle Gardens, Co. Kerry (July). Left: pleasing contrast of colour in buds and flower. Dunloe Castle Gardens, Co. Kerry (July).*

There is a silvery-grey version of *O. rosmarinifolius* known as 'Silve' Jubilee' which, however, lacks the contrasting reddish flower buds and if anything is slightly less hardy. A related species is *O. ledifolius* (with leaves like *Ledum*), which makes a dense compact mound of narrow evergreen, yellowish-green leaves. The flower heads in summer are yellowish brown at first, opening to white with yellowish outer bracts. The whole bush on a hot sunny day has a pleasant honey sweet aroma derived from the yellow gum which covers not only the leaf undersurfaces but the stems as well. So inflammable is this gum in the wild state that this shrub has earned the name 'Kerosene Bush'.

O. ledifolius is only found on the mountains of Tasmania from whence it was first introduced to Britain by the plant hunter Harold Comber in 1928–30. It is a hardier shrub than *O. rosmarinifolius* and can be grown quite successfully on a rock garden or in a patio bed in all but the coldest areas. It enjoys, however, full sun and a well drained soil. All the above are increased by nurserymen from cuttings.

Paeonia suffruticosa 'Joseph Rock'

Paeonia suffruticosa 'Joseph Rock' —
one of the loveliest of all shrubs. Royal
Botanic Gardens, Kew (May).

Of all the plants introduced to western cultivation by Dr. Joseph Rock, the tree peony or Mudan which bears his name is arguably the most beautiful. Rock was an American of Austrian birth who spent a great deal of his life exploring the western provinces of China from Yunnan north to Gansu. He was a man of many talents, a natural linguist, a skilled photographer, an avid collector and a keen student of the border tribes especially the Nakhi of north-west Yunnan. It was on one of his visits to the principality of Choni (now Jone) in south-west Gansu province in the 1920s that Rock discovered the peony growing in a lamasery garden. He was told by the monks that the plant had been dug up in the wild somewhere in the mountains of Gansu. Seed he gathered at the time was sent to America and it is mainly from this introduction that wild *P. suffruticosa* is represented in western gardens today.

Of course, there are garden forms and hybrids too which originated in China and Japan where the Mudan, or 'King of Flowers' as the Chinese call it, has been cultivated for centuries. But lovely though they are, these garden mudans in their varied colours, double as well as single, cannot compare with the wild species as represented by 'Joseph Rock'. Interestingly, Rock was not the first westerner to see this plant. This honour goes to the plant hunters William Purdom and Reginald Farrer who, during their expedition to north-west China in 1924 found a plant similar to, if not the same as that later seen by Rock, growing on a scrub-covered hillside in south Gansu, close to the border with Shaanxi. Farrer's now famous description of this find cannot be bettered. 'There, balancing rarely amid the brushwood, shone out at me the huge expanded goblets of *Paeonia moutan*, refulgent as pure snow and fragrant as heavenly roses. It grew tall and thin and stately, each plant with two or three thin, upstanding wands tipped by the swaying burden of a single upright bloom with a heart of gold, each stainless petal flamed at the base with a clean and definite feathered blotch of maroon.'

For some reason, Farrer did not introduce this plant which makes the Rock introduction all the more valuable. Despite having first arrived in Britain during the 1930s, Rock's peony remains uncommon in cultivation and is one of the most sought after of all shrubs. Its soil requirements are not difficult to meet as it grows equally well on a slightly acid or alkaline soil though good drainage is essential. Although winter hardy, it is easily excited into premature growth in spring and a risk of damage from late frosts.

Except in northern regions, a cool north or west-facing position is held to be preferable to a warm, sheltered, south facing corner. Although subject to competition in its native scrub, Rock's peony in the garden should be given space in which to develop to its full capacity. It is usually seen as a broad, rounded, leafy bush of 1 to 1.2m (3 to 4ft) by as much or more across (the descriptive name *suffruticosa* means sub-shrubby) but given the right conditions it can in time, achieve up to twice this height and a 40 year old specimen of this calibre grows in the garden of Sir Charles and Lady Buchanan at St. Anne's Manor, Sutton Bonington. An equally impressive 50 year old specimen growing in an exposed position in the chalk garden of the late Sir Frederick Stern at Highdown, Sussex is 1.5m (5ft) high and 2m (6ft) across. This specimen regularly produces up to 100 blooms.

Paeonia suffruticosa 'Joseph Rock' –
huge blossoms with dark basal stains.
Royal Botanic Gardens, Kew (May).

A lovely specimen growing in the garden of Lady Anne Palmer at Rosemoor in Devon is 1.2 (4ft) high and as much across after 23 years. This plant has regularly produced up to 30 blooms which in 1983 were increased to 70 creating a magnificent spectacle in early summer. Another fine specimen grows in a border at Kew despite the oft-quoted comment that this peony does do not flourish in the London area due to damage caused to the young growths by spring frost.

Almost all who set eyes on *Paeonia suffruticosa* 'Joseph Rock' in bloom develop an overwhelming desire to have it in their own garden. Unfortunately, it is a plant for which demand far exceeds supply and those who have young plants rarely need to advertise them. It is not an easy plant to increase as fertile seed is rarely produced. Both grafting and layering have proven successful on occasions but until the techniques of micro-propagation or some other breakthrough can change the situation this most desirable of shrubs will remain tantalisingly scarce.

Photinia villosa var. *maximowicziana*

The deciduous species of *Photinia* are an easily grown hardy group of shrubs or occasionally small trees from eastern Asia. Their main requirements in cultivation are a neutral or acid soil, preferably well drained and in sun. While attractive enough in flower and fruit, it is for their rich autumn colour that they are principally grown. The most commonly planted *Photinia villosa* is native to a wide area of China, Korea and Japan, its name referring to the downy nature of the leaves, flower stalks and young shoots (*villosa* meaning covered with soft hairs). It has been in cultivation here since the end of the last century having arrived via Holland. Much less common is a shrub generally treated as a form of *P. villosa* under the name *maximowicziana*, though it is far more distinct than this ranking suggests.

This is a first class, hardy shrub of dense spreading habit to 5m (16ft) or more, high by as much or more across. Trained early in life to a single stem it can attain small tree size and can then be grown and underplanted in a bed or border. Even as a bush it is impressive, with wide-spreading branches down to ground level and it makes a superb specimen in a lawn. Its leaves are rather leathery in texture and boldly veined above, offering a suitable background for the clusters of small

Photinia villosa *var.* maximowicziana – *rich gold autumn foliage. The Hillier Arboretum, Hampshire (November).*

Photinia villosa *var.*
maximowicziana − *generous clusters*
of red fruits in autumn. The Hillier
Arboretum, Hampshire (November).

white flowers which cream the upper-sides of the branches in late spring. These are followed in autumn by orange-red fruits which later ripen to red. At the same time, the leaves turn a rich golden yellow, often with additional red tints. A large bush in full colour is a splendid sight and in my opinion is equal, if not better in this respect, to typical *P. villosa*.

It is a native of Quelpaert (now Cheju Do), an island off the south coast of Korea and was first introduced to western cultivation via Japan in 1897. The first time I set eyes on it was in the Hillier Arboretum in the 1960s and I have seen it in several gardens and private collections since. Nurserymen generally increase this plant from cuttings though it is probably just as easy from seed. The name *maximowicziana*, by the way, commemorates Carl Maximowicz, an eminent Russian botanist and plant collector who travelled extensively in eastern and central Asia during the last century.

× *Phylliopsis hillieri* 'Pinocchio'

Among the many choice dwarf members of the Rhododendron family (*Ericaceae*) which can be grown in acid or peaty soils, the phyllodoces are among the most satisfactory. There are several species available in cultivation, natives of the northern regions of America, Europe and Asia with compact hummocks of narrow, crowded, evergreen, heath-like foliage and terminal clusters of pitcher or bell-shaped flowers ranging in colour from purple or rose to yellow and white. An interesting member of this group is *Phyllodoce breweri*, a Californian

native of the Sierra Nevada in which the richly coloured, purplish–rose bell-shaped flowers are borne in long terminal racemes. This is looser in growth than most other species and does not develop quite the same compact habit.

In the same family as phyllodoce is *Kalmiopsis leacheana*, another dwarf evergreen with equally small, broader leaves, restricted in the wild to the mountains of Oregon in the north west United States. This little shrublet, with its rosy-red, bell-shaped flowers was originally found in the Siskiyou Mountains in 1930 by a Mr. and Mrs. Leach after whom it is named. Interestingly, *Phyllodoce breweri* was also named after the man who first discovered it in 1862, W. H. Brewer.

Nowhere in the wild do the above two plants come together, but in cultivation, they are often grown in the same peat garden or in the same nursery bed. It was in such a place, the now defunct nursery of Messers Hillier at Chandlers Ford in Hampshire, that a hybrid between the two was discovered in about 1960. Since then it has been propagated and distributed fairly widely so that it is now available from several specialist nurserymen. It was named × *Phylliopsis hillieri* in recognition of its origin, the name *Phylliopsis* combining the names of its parents *Phyllodoce* and *Kalmiopsis*. To distinguish the Chandlers Ford seedling from others of the same parentage it was given the name 'Pinocchio' after the bright and cheerful little puppet of that name who was brought to life with a touch of magic.

× *Phylliopsis hillieri* 'Pinocchio' is a dwarf, hardy, evergreen shrublet up to 30cm (12in), forming tuffets and hummocks of small flattened leaves. The bell-shaped reddish-purple flowers are borne in terminal racemes during late spring at which time the plant is a bright and

× Phylliopsis hillieri *'Pinocchio' — a choice dwarf evergreen for lime-free soils. Glendoick Gardens, Perthshire (April).*

charming member of the peat bed community. A cool, peaty, well-drained position in sun or dappled shade seems to suit it best though it had proved remarkably adaptable to relatively drier gardens, more so than either of its parents. Indeed, a plant thrives in my garden on an acid sand which dries to a dust-like consistency in most summers.

If it has one weakness, 'Pinocchio' is apt to flower itself to death. Often, every shoot bears flowers, necessitating a careful pruning immediately after flowering. Apart from initiating new growth, this also helps to keep the plant neat and compact in habit. There are now other × *Phylliopsis hybrids* in cultivation, one of which has been named 'Coppelia'. This is the result of a deliberate cross between *Phyllodoce empetriformis* and a different form of *Kalmiopsis leacheana* to the one which resulted in 'Pinocchio'. It was made in 1977 by Barry Starling, a skilled cultivator and an authority on dwarf, peat-loving shrubs. Not unlike 'Pinocchio' in habit, it has bell-shaped, lavender-pink flowers in compact terminal racemes in late spring. Mr Starling chose to name his plant after the beautiful doll, Coppelia, of Hoffman's legend and Delibes ballet who was a deliberate creation of an eccentric toymaker, Dr. Coppelius. All forms of × *Phylliopsis* are increased by nurserymen from cuttings.

Prostanthera cuneata

The mint bushes *Prostanthera* species of Australia are so-called because many of them give off a mint-like aroma when bruised. This is perhaps not surprising since they belong to the same family as the mint (*Labiatae*) having the characteristic square stems and two lipped flowers. There are several species in British cultivation, tender shrubs with abundant purple flowers, best suited to the cool greenhouse or

Prostanthera cuneata – low evergreen mounds of dark green aromatic foliage. Author's garden, Hampshire (June).

Prostanthera cuneata – *flowers attractively marked within. Author's garden, Hampshire (June).*

conservatory. *P. cuneata*, the Alpine mint bush, however, is a remarkable exception. In the wild it is found in the mountains of south-east Australia, including Tasmania, where it grows into a dome-shaped bush to 1m (3ft) high and 1.5m (5ft) across. The tiny dark evergreen leaves have a wedge-shaped base (hence the name *cuneata*) and densely crowd the shoots, smelling when bruised, not of mint but of wintergreen.

In cultivation it blooms in the summer, the bell-shaped, two lipped flowers 2cm (¾in) across, white with a pretty pattern of yellow and purple spots in the throat. The flowers are carried in short racemes, crowding the young shoots and contrasting effectively with the dark foliage. Five years ago I was offered a plant of *Prostanthera cuneata* for my garden and knowing the tender nature of these plants I was dubious about accepting. The donor, Peter Chappell, who gardens in the New Forest, assured me, however, that this was an exception to the rule so I planted it in my acid sand. It has never looked back and despite three severe winters in a row, has suffered no damage whatsoever.

I have seen it in many gardens over the last few years and it would appear to be hardy in the southern and western areas of Britain certainly and in warm pockets elsewhere. More recently I saw a large plant in a garden in the Lake District, not in a sheltered woodland garden but on a wind-swept mountainside where it thrived. Given full sun and a well-drained soil it is a shrub worth trying outside in all but the coldest places. Being dwarf, it is ideal for the small garden and particularly suitable for a patio bed. It is increased by nurserymen from cuttings.

Rhododendron bureavii

One of the great advantages of gardening on acid soils is the range of rhododendrons one can grow. True, there are some species which are relatively tolerant of alkaline soils but the majority abhor them. *Rhododendron bureavii* is one such, a shapely species which in some situations and certainly in the wild can reach tree-like proportions but is normally seen in cultivation as a shrub of compact habit up to 3m (9ft). The flowers are tubular, bell-shaped, flared at the mouth and vary in colour from white flushed pink to rose speckled crimson or purple

within. They are borne in loosely rounded trusses of 10 to 20 from the tips of the branches in late spring.

Attractive enough in flower, it is for its leaves that *R. bureavii* is most usually grown. In this respect it is one of the most handsome of all rhododendrons. They are leathery in texture, 7.5 to 12.5cm (3 to 5in) long, glossy dark green above and covered beneath as are the young shoots and leaf stalks with a dense woolly pelt of rust-red hairs. On the young leaves, the hairs are salmon pink but they soon darken to the rich colour of the mature leaf.

It is a hardy and easily-grown rhododendron, its slow growth and compact habit making it suitable for the smaller garden where it will eventually become a dominant and much admired feature. Because of its main attraction, it needs to be given an open position away from larger, more vigorous shrubs and for that matter, dense shade. Like most of its kind it does not care for dryness at the roots.

R. bureavii is native to northern Yunnan in south-west China where it grows in open pine forests and rhododendron thickets in the mountains. It was first discovered by a famous French missionary, the Abbé Delavay, in 1896 and is named after E. Bureau (1830–1918), a French professor. It can be increased from seed with varying results (often pleasing) but selected forms are normally grafted.

Opposite: Rhododendron bureavii – *handsome foliage and flowers. Exbury Gardens, Hampshire (May).*

Rhododendron macabeanum

In the wild, *Rhododendron macabeanum* is more of a bushy tree than a shrub and the same can be said for many of the older specimens in cultivation. It is not, however, fast growing and there are many smaller shrubby flowering specimens to be seen. Indeed, a specimen of some 3

Rhododendron macabeanum – *an old specimen at its peak. Trewithen Gardens, Cornwall (March).*

Rhododendron macabeanum – *dense rounded trusses of a rich yellow. Trewithen Gardens, Cornwall (March).*

× 3m (9 × 9ft) grows on the acid sand of a relatively small garden near my home in Hampshire and has flowered fairly regularly for the last eight or nine years, each year seeing an increase in the number of flower trusses.

Even as a young non-flowering specimen, *R. macabeanum* is worth growing for its large leathery leaves of up to 30cm (12in) long and 15 to 22cm (6 to 9in) wide. These are dark green and shining above and covered beneath with a dense suede-like pelt of hairs which varies in colour from white to grey or fawn. As the plant ages, the leaves are increasingly carried towards the ends of the branches where they form impressive clusters. The flowers are normally borne in dense globular trusses in early spring. Individually these are tubular bell-shaped, 7.5cm (3in) long and vary in colour from pale sulphur (sometimes ivory-white) to a deep yellow with a purple blotch in the throat. The young growths in spring are also worthy of attention rising from the ends of the branches like grey candles with red trimmings.

It is native to north-east India (Nagaland and Manipur) and was first discovered on Mount Japro in 1882 by Sir George Watt who named it after Mr. M'Cabe, Deputy Commissioner for the Naga Hills, who gave him assistance during his travels in the area. In the wild it is said to form dense stands on the summits of hills as well as being scattered through mixed woodlands. All the older plants in cultivation, however, are the result of seeds collected in the same location in 1927 by the plant hunter Frank Kingdon Ward. It is hardy in all but the coldest areas of the cool temperate zones and is one of the best of the large leaved rhododendrons for general cultivation being more tolerant than most of drought, wind and frost.

Although there is a fine specimen flourishing in the Royal Botanic Garden, Edinburgh, some of the best specimens are found in the woodland gardens in the West of Scotland and in Cornwall. At Trewithen in the latter county, there is a particularly fine deep yellow flowered form of *R. macabeanum*, grown from Kingdon Ward's original 1927 seed. When last measured in 1974, it had attained 7×10.6m (23×35ft) across. It was about this time that I saw it on a cold spring morning in full flower with hundreds of trusses in peak condition. *R. macabeanum* can easily be raised from seed but selected forms are grafted by nurserymen.

Robinia hispida

Most gardeners are familiar with the False Acacia or Black Locust *Robinia pseudacacia*. It is perhaps the most ubiquitous of North American trees, planted by the million in northern temperate zones and running wild whenever conditions are suitable. It has its good points, of course, and there are several, but it is a tree one would need to think carefully about before planting it in the garden. One need have no such qualms however, about the Rose Acacia *Robinia hispida* which,

Robinia hispida – *ample clusters of rich pink pea-flowers. Jenkyn Place, Hampshire (June).*

although it suckers vigorously in the wild in the mountains of Tennessee and elsewhere, maintains a quiet profile in the garden.

It is a loose growing shrub whose stems, unlike those of the False Acacia, are thornless. They are, however, densely covered with gland-tipped bristles which glisten red on the young growths. Indeed, this character is referred to in the descriptive name, *hispida* meaning 'bristly'. Nurserymen commonly graft this shrub onto False Acacia stock and train it as a small tree. Although small tree specimens, with the help of a stake or similar support, can look very pretty in an enclosed garden or courtyard, the site needs to be quite sheltered lest winds break the brittle branches. Failing this, the Rose Acacia is best treated as a shrub and trained against a wall or fence. Even then, strong winds can sometimes cause damage to the long shoots, especially when heavy with flowers.

The flowers are shaped like those of a small sweet pea, in colour a lovely deep rose shade with a small yellow flash on the inside of the standard. They are carried in loose drooping clusters in early summer from the previous year's shoots, contrasting effectively with the dark green, ash-like leaves.

Although first introduced as along ago as 1743, the Rose Acacia is not common in British cultivation where it is usually found in sunny courtyards and wall gardens. Sun and warmth and a well-drained acid or alkaline soil are its main requirements, given which it will flower quite freely while covering a large area of wall. The largest specimen I have seen occupied an area of 3sq m (9sq ft) on a south-facing wall in Hampshire. It is particularly happy in relatively drier and south eastern areas.

Rosa moyesii 'Geranium'

There are many plants named after people who had no particular interest in the subject. One of these *Rosa moyesii* is named after the Rev. J. Moyes, a missionary in western China and known to the plant hunter E. H. Wilson who first introduced this rose to England in 1903. Whether Moyes fully appreciated his place in botanical posterity is not recorded nor is there any evidence to suggest that he eventually returned home to cultivate and enjoy his namesake, that would have been an appropriate, if unlikely, ending. What is certain though is that *Rosa moyesii* from its first introduction was accepted by gardeners as being among the élite of its kind.

It is a robust shrub with strong, erect, pale-thorned stems 2.5 to 3m (7 to 9ft) high, or occasionally more, and as much across at its top. The leaves are composed of 7 to 13 dark green, toothed leaflets while the flowers in the best forms are a striking blood red in colour with a central boss of creamy stamens. These are 5 to 6.5cm (2 to 2½in) across and borne singly or sometimes in pairs on short laterals along the older branches in late spring and early summer. They are followed by an abundance of bottle-shaped, brilliant, scarlet heps which ripen through autumn into early winter. It is a hardy rose suitable for most any soil in full sun. Its leggy habit is a weakness but this is easily overcome by planting low-growing shrubs or perennials to help conceal its base.

Rosa moyesii makes a stunning centre-piece in plantings of other shrub roses or it may be planted alone or in groups in an island bed in the lawn. Some people place it at the back of a border where its beauty

(but not its bare lower stems) can be seen above neighbouring planting. No other rose in my opinion compares with the colour of *R. moyesii* except perhaps 'Geranium' raised in the Royal Horticultural Society's Garden at Wisley, Surrey in about 1937. This is more compact and bushy in habit, with lighter green leaves, slightly larger heps and flowers of geranium red, lighter, however, than those of typical *R. moyesii*.

'Geranium' is perhaps, the best form of the species for general cultivation and is worth considering for all but the smallest gardens. Wilson collected seed of *R. moyesii* near Tachienlu (now Kangding) in west Sichuan, the 'Gateway to Tibet" as it was then known. It had already been found in the same location some years earlier by the English naturalist A. E. Pratt. In 1981, I had the privilege of visiting this area during a botanical trek to the Tibetan border. I found the mountain slopes and ravines covered in dense scrub in which many roses flourished. One of these was *R. moyesii* and seed I collected at the time produced a number of strong growing plants. When these began to flower four years later the flowers, instead of being blood-red, were rich pink. Such forms however are not uncommon in the wild and one of these, 'Fargesii', is available in cultivation.

R. moyesii and its forms may be grown from seed but selected forms are increased by nurserymen by grafting or budding.

Rosa moyesii 'Geranium' – flowers of glowing red. Jenkyn Place, Hampshire (June).

Rubus biflorus

Rubus biflorus – *ghostly white stems in winter. Cambridge University Botanic Garden (February).*

My two years as a student gardener at the Cambridge Botanic Garden remains one of the most exciting and enjoyable periods of my life. Not only was my enthusiasm fired by the teachings of the staff under its Director the late John Gilmour, but my plant horizons were considerably expanded by the huge, living collections the garden contained. One of my favourite, though unofficial, pastimes, was to visit the Winter Garden at night with a torch to pick out in its bright beam the coloured barks and stems of the dogwoods, willows and brambles. Naturally, winter was the best time for this activity, when the stems stood leafless and stark in the darkness.

Several brambles were grown at that time for their white or blue-bloomy stems, but none in my opinion could compare with, let alone surpass, those of *Rubus biflorus*, a native of the Himalayas and China. Who cared that the leaves were of no merit nor indeed were the flowers (*biflorus* meaning flowers in twos) and small yellow raspberries, though these were at least edible? The one and only reason for its presence in cultivation is its 'whitewashed' stems which can take on a ghostly effect when visibility is down. I was reminded of this some ten years later when scrambling across a mountainside in east Nepal, during my first plant-hunting expedition. My colleagues and I had lost our way in a bamboo forest at the end of a long gruelling day. The light was fading as we fought our way through a dense thicket of secondary growth in which the white prickly stems of *Rubus biflorus* clawed at us like the arms of some ghostly octopus, seriously impeding our progress. It is an experience I am unlikely to forget, though I hasten to add that it did not change my mind about its ornamental merits.

It is hardy and easy to grow in most acid or alkaline soils and needs plenty of room in which to develop to its full potential which may be anything from 2 to 3m (6 to 9ft) high, by as much across. It forms a stout clump of suckering stems which need to be pruned to the base before, or immediately after, flowering. Bearing in mind that it is the winter effect of the young stems that is required, once winter is passed and the leaves develop, the older stems can be discarded. *R. biflorus* is particularly effective underplanted with winter aconites or winter flowering heaths (*Erica carnea* and *E. × darleyensis*).

Nurserymen increase this bramble either by cuttings or division, the latter being a relatively simple, though potentially hazardous job.

Climbers

Actinidia kolomikta

The first time I saw *Actinidia kolomikta*, I thought it the most spectacular flowering climber I had ever seen. It was an old specimen covering a large area of a west-facing wall and was the first plant to catch my eye as I approached the house along the front drive. When I finally confronted the plant, however, I realized that the 'flowers' I had admired from afar were not flowers at all but leaves. It is the leaves that make this climber so desirable. Heart-shaped and thin-textured, they are quite large, 7.5 to 15cm (3 to 6in) long, varying to a remarkable degree in their colouration. Some are plain green while others carry varying proportions of white or pink. Some leaves are tricoloured (green, pink and white), the overall effect being reminiscent of a painter's palette or a colourful tapestry.

Being a deciduous climber, the leaf display varies each year but providing it has not been planted in heavy shade it is a totally reliable feature. Although often slow initially, it soon grows away when established, its long slender rich brown, twining shoots reaching in time 7m (22ft), or more, given support.

Actinidia kolomikta – *like a painter's palette from a distance. Kiftsgate Court, Gloucestershire (June).*

Actinidia kolomikta – *leaves of three colours. Cambridge University Botanic Garden (June).*

It is a native to north-east Asia and Japan from whence it was first introduced by Charles Maries in 1877. In the wild it grows in woodland where its dense network of stems casts a net over shrubs and small trees and climbs into the lower branches of taller trees. In 1984 I saw this plant wild in the mixed conifer and deciduous forests of the Changbai Mountains in north-east China. Here, it grew in clearings and stream gullies in semi-shade, its stems scrambling into trees and often hanging free in multicoloured curtains. It can be grown into trees in the garden so long as it is planted away from the dry zone at the tree's base. Ideally, it should be planted beneath the periphery of the branches and trained into the canopy via a cane or similar support. Old trees are the best vehicles to choose, especially those of limited ornamental value and with low branches.

More commonly it is planted against a wall on a wire support. One sometimes reads that it grows best on a west-facing wall but I have seen thriving specimens on both north and east-facing walls and when one considers the cool, partially shaded conditions of its native woods this should come as no surprise. I believe shelter from cold winds to be a key to success with this plant as I have never seen it thriving in a cold exposed situation in the wild.

Given a suitable site, it seems indifferent to acid or alkaline soil so long as it is moist and well drained. One needs patience in its early years until it is sufficiently established to make the most of its support. It should also be given protection – especially as a youngster – against the close attentions of cats who find the smell of the leaves and stems strangely fascinating. A keen gardener and cat lover once told me that she had to replant a young specimen several times until it dawned on her who the culprits were.

The flowers of *Actinidia kolomikta* are 1.5cm ($\frac{1}{2}$in) across, white, fragrant and produced in clusters from the axils of the leaves in June. The small, edible, greenish-yellow fruits are rarely produced in Britain lacking no doubt, consistent summer heat.

The varied leaf colours generally begin to attract when plants are a few years old and are at their most impressive on mature plants. The descriptive name *kolomikta* is the native name for this plant in the Amur Region of south-east Siberia. It is increased by nurserymen from cuttings.

Dregea sinensis

One of my favourite greenhouse plants when I worked on a north of England Parks Department as a young man, was *Hoya carnosa*. An evergreen twining climber, it was the tight umbels of star-like, pale almond, pink-tinted flowers that most attracted me, especially when they exuded sweet drops of nectar which I loved to touch with my fingers, transferring the sweet smear to my tongue.

Dregea sinensis – *delicously fragrant star-like flowers. Jenkyn Place, Hampshire (July).*

It is a member of a large group known as the Milkweed family (*Asclepiadaceae*), so named because of the sticky milky-white juice and the abundance, in the wild in North America, of certain herbaceous members of the family. One only has to scrape the stem or pick a leaf of this climber for the sap to come welling from the broken surface. A native of Australia where it is known as the Wax Plant, this climber requires a heated greenhouse in which to thrive in Britain but *Dregea sinensis*, a relative of *Hoya* is hardy at least in the warmer regions where it is occasionally seen trained to a south or west-facing wall reaching in height as much as 3 to 4m (9 to 13ft). It is a deciduous climber, its slender twining, downy stems fastening on to whatever support is provided and bearing pairs of slender-pointed, heart-shaped leaves, velvety-downy beneath.

The flowers appear in summer in slender-stalked nodding clusters. The individual flowers are star shaped, a little over 1.5cm ($\frac{1}{2}$in) across and fragrant. Basically, they are white or creamy white, with a central zone of reddish spots and streaks. They are remarkably like those of *Hoya carnosa* but lack the waxy texture while the nectar is never as freely produced as it is in that plant. *Dregea sinensis* may be regarded as a near hardy version of the Wax Plant and is certainly worth considering by gardeners with a warm sunny wall to offer. If the soil is well drained then all the better.

It is native to central China and was first discovered by the Irish plant collector Augustine Henry in the hills above the Yangtze city of Yichang in 1887. Ten years later, it was introduced from the same location by E. H. Wilson then employed by the Arnold Arboretum, Massachusetts. In the summer of 1983 while visiting the Wudang Mountains, north of Yichang, I saw *Dregea sinensis* scrambling into the canopies of small trees and shrubs. It was especially plentiful in ravines where the stony slopes made for good drainage and the sun created hot, dry conditions. It grew in thickets, sharing its home with *Kolkwitzia amabilis*, the Beauty Bush, as well as various roses and indigoferas.

One of the finest specimens I know has flourished for many years on the south facing wall of Jenkyn Place at Bentley in Hampshire. There it is trained to a framework of wire, its roots in the dry rubble soil at the wall's base. It receives plenty of sun during a normal summer and in addition basks in the warmth reflected from a patio at its base. Most years its stems are freely hung with the pretty flower-clusters whose delicious fragrance wafts gently through any open window or door. The descriptive name *sinensis*, meaning 'of China', refers to its origin. It is also sometimes referred to as *Wattakaka sinensis*. It is increased by nurserymen by seed when available or from cuttings.

Lapageria rosea

Many years ago, as a gardening apprentice on a visit to a city-owned park in the north of England, I had occasion to open the door of a rather neglected conservatory leaning against the wall of a large Victorian house. The park had previously been a privately owned estate with a substantial area of garden around the family home. The glass panes in the cast-iron structure were heavily stained with green algae, further weakening the light which filtered through the rain-clouds above. Peering through the gloom I saw the untidy dark mass of an evergreen climber trained to the wall, its long twining stems

Lapageria rosea — *exotic-flowered climber for a sheltered wall. Caragh Lough, Co. Kerry (August).*

groping their way along the bars of the ventilation system. If I had merely glanced and retreated I would have missed an experience to remember the rest of my life.

Fortunately, I stepped through the door and ventured beneath the all-enveloping embrace of the climber. My eyes opened wide, for hanging from the dark canopy were scores of the most exotic looking waxy bells of a rich crimson colour with a faint rose marbling. Never having seen it before I had not the faintest idea as to the identity of this marvellous flower, but a friend of mine, a keen plantsman, was able to enlighten me. It was my first encounter with the Chilean Bellflower — *Lapageria rosea*. The name *rosea* refers to the flower colour while the generic name was given in honour of the Empress Josephine of France, a keen botanist and first wife of Napoleon Bonaparte, whose maiden name was de la Pagerie.

Lapageria rosea – the rich colour of its waxen bells. Caragh Lough, Co. Kerry (August).

It is a most distinctive plant both botanically and ornamentally. Its few close relatives share the same shady, damp, mountain forest conditions in its native Chile where it is known by the name 'Copihue' and it is also found in similar places across the border in Argentina. Named from a dried specimen around the turn of the 19th century, it was first seen in western cultivation in 1847 as one of a number of ornamental plants brought home from his second South American expedition by the Cornishman William Lobb. It was marketed by Lobb's employers, the Veitch Nursery of Exeter, and quickly became one of the most admired and sought after inhabitants of Victorian conservatories.

It is in conservatories and greenhouses that it is mostly seen today for although it will take some frost, it does not care for really cold winters nor, for that matter, exposure to drying winds or hot sun. It is occasionally seen flourishing out of doors in the milder, wetter areas of the cool temperate zones.

The flowers can vary in size and depth of colour and named selections are sometimes available. A pure white form is one of the most beautiful and desirable while another is 'Nash Court', whose flowers are soft pink with a slight marbling. A greater number of selections are grown in Chile whose national flower it is. Flowers apart, the Chilean Bellflower is an uninspiring, some would even say ugly plant with long stiff shoots of 4.5m (15ft) or more. The leaves, too, are stiff, glossy dark green and leathery, with a slender point and few veins. It grows best in a deep acid loam in which its roots can wander to their hearts' content. Shade, gentle warmth and support for its twining stems are other requirements if it is to flourish. It is propagated by nurserymen from cuttings or by seed when available, though the latter method is of no use should selected forms be required. It may also be increased by layering.

Mutisia oligodon

When I first saw this unusual and attractive climber flowering in the Hillier Arboretum in 1964, I was told by a colleague that it was, in effect, a climbing pink, evergreen daisy. Treading on that humble herb of lawns at the time I could see the likeness in flower form but decided that all comparison ended there. Both daisy and mutisia are members of the same vast family (*Compositae*) which also includes such apparently disparate members as the thistle, dandelion and golden rod. The daisy, however, is a well known British native, while *Mutisia oligodon* is a rare plant from the Andes of Chile and Argentina from whence it was first introduced by Harold Comber in 1925–27.

It is a low growing suckering plant with numerous scrambling, ribbed stems, clothed with stalkless coarsely toothed leaves up to 4cm (1½in) long which end in a long slender tendril. By this means the stems clamber into any support to hand. The flower-heads, which have been likened to those of a gazania, are borne singly on slender stalks from the tips of the shoots. They are quite large, 5 to 7.5cm (2 to 3in) across, with a ring of salmon-pink petals (ray florets) and are produced continuously throughout summer and intermittently into autumn.

M. oligodon has a rather untidy habit which is best accommodated by planting it near a small twiggy shrub through which it can scramble and will eventually swamp. Alternatively, it can be trained up a wire

Opposite: Mutisia oligodon – *masses of large, pink, daisy flowers. The Hillier Arboretum, Hampshire (July).*

frame where it will reach no more than 2m (6ft), if that. Such a plant once grew on the south-facing wall of Jermyns House, home of the late Sir Harold Hillier, near Romsey in Hampshire. This plant flourished for many years and each summer its flowers were a constant source of interest to visitors. One very special visitor in the late 1960s was Harold Comber, whom I had the pleasure of taking round the Arboretum – an unforgettable experience as so many of his introductions were then being grown there. On approaching the mutisia, he asked me if I had seen the plant nod its flower heads. When I naively said no he laughed and explained that it was an old friend having been introduced by him from the Andes where it formed large, low suckering colonies on dry, rocky slopes. He reckoned that it would take all the sun we could give it and that provided it was given good drainage, it should flourish indefinitely.

It certainly enjoyed being in the rubble and acid, sandy soil at the base of the wall and could not have been given a warmer, sunnier pocket. Sadly, this plant perished after being dug up during a building operation many years later but fortunately not before propagation material had been secured.

Although *M. oligodon* is said to be the hardiest of its clan, there is no doubt that it grows best in mild areas and in sheltered gardens elsewhere. Being relatively small, it can easily be given winter protection, if necessary, otherwise, in cold areas it is worth considering as a cool greenhouse or conservatory subject. Another point made to me by Harold Comber concerning this plant is that in the wild it often established itself among rocks and boulders, its stems filling the spaces in-between. This condition can be emulated in gardens by placing large stones on the soil surface around the base of the plant. Certainly, a well-established and flourishing colony of this plant once grew at the base of a low dry stone wall of a famous garden in Devon. It was so at home that its stems scrambled up and over the wall to create what some visitors at first glance thought to be a hedge.

The name *oligodon*, meaning 'few-toothed', refers to the leaves. It is increased by nurserymen from cuttings or when available, from seed.

Rosa bracteata

On the south-facing wall of my home grows a plant of *Rosa bracteata*, the Macartney Rose. It was grown from seed sent to me by a friend at the Shanghai Botanic Garden in 1982. The information on the seed packet told me that it had been collected in the wild in Checkiang (now Zhejiang) Province the previous year. I had no trouble in germinating the seed and the plant on my wall is the only one retained, the rest I gave away. It flowered for the first time in 1984 and each year since it has delighted me in summer and autumn with a succession of fragrant flowers up to 10cm (4in) across, the white petals an ideal backing for the bold boss of golden stamens. Although they are produced singly, the flowers are well distributed and while at no time is the plant covered with blossom they appear over an extended period until the first frosts of autumn, making them a valuable asset.

In the wild, *R. bracteata* enjoys relatively warm conditions and not surprisingly it is only suitable for the milder areas and even here is best given a warm wall. It is more of a scandent shrub than a true climber and its stout, densely hairy and viciously thorny stems need the support

of a wire frame up which to clamber. In warm areas, I have seen it as a free-standing bush but it needs plenty of room in which to spread.

Its leaves are normally evergreen and a dark lustrous green above which is a large part of its attraction. However, even in warm areas, unusually severe winters turn them brown and my plant in January is usually a wretched sight. Not only the leaves, but the young shoots, too, are killed when temperatures are plummetting and freezing winds persist. One of the problems is that in an insular climate such as Britain's, growth continues well into autumn with no chance to ripen before winter. Fortunately, with the warmth of spring, new shoots emerge from the old wood and by mid-summer the whole plant is full of lush growth again. My plant would now be 3m (9ft) high and as much across if I did not prune it each year in spring to half this. The flowers, being borne on the current year's growth, means that I do not miss out on the season's display.

Given sufficient space and ideal conditions, this rose can reach 7m (22ft) and as much across creating an impressive picture in summer. Apart from full sun and plenty of warmth, it enjoys a well-drained soil and is ideally suited for the sheltered, sunny courtyard or patio garden where reflected heat will prove much to its liking.

The name *bracteata* is a reference to the large, downy, feathery bracts (leaflike appendages) which surround the short flower stalk. This rose

Rosa bracteata – *large flowers produced over a long period. Author's garden, Hampshire (July).*

Opposite: Solanum crispum
'Glasnevin' – one of the longest
flowering of all climbers. Stockbridge,
Hampshire (July).

was first introduced to England in 1793 by Lord Macartney, hence the
common name. In truth its collector is likely to have been John
Haxton, a gardener accompanying Lord Macartney's Embassy to the
Chinese Emperor. Haxton was employed by another member of the
Embassy, Sir George Staunton, who is recorded as having presented a
plant to Kew Gardens. Interestingly, Haxton is said to have acquired his
plant in Chekiang (Zhejiang) Province, from whence came my seed.

R. *bracteata*, crossed with a yellow Tea Rose by W. Paul in 1917,
produced 'Mermaid', one of the most remarkable of all roses for a large
wall. It inherits the vigour and leaves of the Macartney rose while its
large, pale yellow flowers are likewise born over a long period. It also
does best on a south or west-facing wall. *Rosa bracteata* is increased by
nurserymen from cuttings or by grafting and when seed is available it is
normally easy to germinate.

Solanum crispum 'Glasnevin'

When non botanically-minded gardeners first set eyes upon *Solanum
crispum* they often find it hard to believe that this scandent evergreen
shrub can be related to the potato and the tomato. The answer, of
course, lies mainly in the flower and on closer examination the family
likeness is soon apparent in the five-lobed, star-like flower and the
central 'beak' of yellow stamens. The green, ripening to yellowish-
white, fruits are also similar though small and of little ornamental merit.

Solanum crispum is native to Chile and Peru and was first introduced
to cultivation as long ago as 1830. It is a sun-loving plant producing

*Solanum crispum 'Glasnevin' – the
flowers show its kinship with the potato
and tomato. Author's garden,
Hampshire (August).*

long green, shortly downy shoots which can reach as much as 9m (30ft) or more in an ideal situation. The leaves are pointed and shining dark green above remaining on the stems except in cold winters. Their margins are wavy hence the descriptive name *crispum*. The fragrant flowers of various shades of blue, some 2.5 to 3cm (1 to 1¼in) across, are borne in large branched clusters from the current year's growths. They are produced continuously on the growing shoots from late spring to early autumn.

Even better is 'Glasnevin', sometimes incorrectly referred to as 'Autumnale', a selection first distributed by the National Botanic Garden, Glasnevin, Dublin in the early years of this century. This is the form most commonly cultivated and excels in its royal blue flowers, bluish-purple towards the centre and in its longer flowering period which extends well into autumn. In mild areas or in a cool greenhouse or conservatory, 'Glasnevin' continues producing flowers into winter and the last flowers I enjoyed on a plant growing by my front door in 1986 were still apparent two weeks before Christmas. It is also said to be even more vigorous in growth than *S. crispum*, if that is possible.

For abundance and continuous flowering, 'Glasnevin' takes some beating, added to which the exotic nature of the flowers bring a touch of Mediterranean or sub-tropical climes to one's garden. The one drawback is its lack of hardiness in cold areas. It needs sun and warmth and I have seen plants growing and flowering on sunny sheltered walls in inner-city areas where reflected warmth is beneficial to the cultivation of semi-hardy plants. I have two plants in my own garden in Hampshire, one in a border open to the south-east, another on a west-facing wall by my porch. During the low winter temperatures of recent years, the former plant has been defoliated and twice cut to the ground while the other plant has escaped with some loss of leaf and damage to growing tips of the unripened shoots. Plants severely damaged by frosts can be pruned to the ground in spring and as long as they are well established they will sprout again, none the worse for their ordeal.

Solanum crispum 'Glasnevin' is not fussy as to soil, acid or alkaline, though a good drainage is an asset during cold wet winters. The main problem with a well established plant in a good site is to control its vigour. The expanding shoots can be threaded through or loosely tied to wires fixed to a wall or fence or, alternatively, trained over a shed or garage roof to create an exotic cap of purple blossom the summer through. While *S. crispum* itself can be grown from seed when available, selected forms including 'Glasnevin' are increased by nurserymen from cuttings.

Tropaeolum speciosum

If there is one hardy climber which in full flower is guaranteed to attract instant attention it is the Scotch Flame Flower or Scotch Creeper *Tropaeolum speciosum*. Related to the well-known annual 'Nasturtium' (*T. majus*), this is an herbaceous perennial whose slender stems rise each year in summer from fleshy stick-like, underground rhizomes. The emerald green leaves are rounded and divided to the base into several finger-like lobes while their stalks are long and flexible, twining round suitable support, so enabling the stems to haul themselves off the ground. The long stalked, long spurred flowers are a brilliant scarlet

Opposite: Tropaeolum speciosum – *brilliantly coloured flowers in summer. The Gables, Shropshire (July).*

with a yellow throat and stamens and throughout late summer months are borne in profusion along the stems, clear of the leaves. These are replaced by equally attractive berries which mature from green to a rich indigo.

In the wild, *T. speciosum*, which name, by the way, means 'showy', is native to the moist mountain forests of southern Chile and the island of Chiloe from whence it was first introduced to cultivation by William Lobb in 1846. It is a relatively hardy plant though, not surprisingly considering its native habitat, it is seen at its best in the cooler summers and moister conditions found on the Pacific coast of North America and in northern and western areas of Britain, hence the name Scotch Creeper. It commonly occurs in Scottish gardens in some of which it has become an ineradicable, though beautiful, weed. In relatively drier southern areas, it is less rampant though just as spectacular when planted in shade or against a sheltered north or east-facing wall up which it will scramble if supporting wires are provided.

It is often planted among evergreen azaleas where its roots and lower stems are cool and shaded while its flowering growth clothes the canopy above. Elsewhere, especially in the north, it is commonly planted beneath hedges (though not too close to the dry root zone) where its numerous stems create extensive nets or blankets of growth over the outside of the canopy. It is particularly effective when grown over conifer hedges such as Lawson cypress and is exceptional on yew, the blackish-green foliage of this evergreen providing an ideal backing to the emerald green and scarlet of the climber. One such combination I remember had the Scotch Creeper forming an intricate tracery to a height of 7m (22ft). From a distance its flowers seemed to create a conspicuous red stain on the dark hedge.

Tropaeolum speciosum demands a moist but well drained acid or peaty soil for maximum effort while heavy clays and soils which dry out in summer should be avoided. Its rhizomes should be planted 7.5cm (3in) or more deep, laid horizontally taking care not to break them. Alternatively, it can be planted already established from pots. It is increased by nurserymen from seed or root cuttings though the latter are not easy to establish.

Conifers

Juniperus conferta

Japan like Britain is blessed with a wide variety of coastal topography from mountains and cliffs to sand dunes, shingle banks and salt marsh. It also supports a variety of junipers whereas in Britain there are only two, *Juniperus communis* and its prostrate variety *montana*. The last named I have seen forming mats and curtains of tight growth on the sea cliffs of Caithness in Scotland and it maintains this habit when brought into cultivation. Japan, too, has its prostrate seashore junipers, three in all of which *J. conferta* is one of the most useful in the garden. In the wild it grows on sand dunes and on sandy seashores where it often forms extensive carpets of prickly growth.

It was first introduced from the wild into western cultivation by E. H. Wilson in 1914 but it has never been as common as its merit

Juniperus conferta – splashed with the blood red leaves of a maple. Knightshayes Court, Devon (November).

deserves. In cultivation it maintains its naturally low carpeted habit, its shortly ascending shoots crowded with needle-like, pale glossy-green leaves marked with a white band above. It is suited to most soils, especially those well drained or of a sandy nature, and makes a useful ground cover beneath trees so long as the shade is not too heavy. It is also useful for planting on banks or wall tops where its stems can trail down steep or vertical surfaces. One particularly inspired piece of planting I have seen has it forming a carpet beneath a Korean maple (*Acer palmatum* var. *coreanum*). One autumn, some years ago, I saw this juniper spattered with the fallen maple leaves which were blood red on green, a striking contrast. Later of course, the dead leaves would be cleared away.

Juniperus conferta – dense, evergreen carpets of sharp pointed leaves. Valley Gardens, Windsor Great Park, Berkshire (November).

J. conferta is also worth growing in coastal areas where its salt tolerance should be an asset. Several selections have been made in North-America including 'Blue Pacific' with blue-green foliage, 'Boulevard' which is very prostrate and 'Emerald Sea' which has emerald green foliage during summer and autumn and is said to be very salt tolerant. Of the three, only 'Blue Pacific' is readily available in Britain.

J. conferta, which name means crowded (a reference to the leaves), is increased by nurserymen from cuttings.

Microbiota decussata

It might seem unusual that such an ornamental and botanically interesting conifer as *Microbiota decussata* should remain unseen by western travellers and botanists until 1921. The reason for this is that it is found in a relatively isolated area of south east Siberia, somewhere to the east of Vladivostock. It grows there on mountains above the timber line where it is said to be quite common. Having been discovered by a Russian botanist called Komarov it was first cultivated in the Botanic Garden at Tashkent in Central Asia. Not until the 1960s, however, did it arrive in west European cultivation via Czechoslovakia.

Botanically, it is a distinct plant with affinities to both juniper and the *arbor vitae* (*Thuja*). Indeed, its similarity to *Thuja orientalis* (sometimes treated as *Biota orientalis*) is referred to in its first (generic) name *Microbiota* meaning 'small *Biota*'. Its descriptive name *decussata* refers to the leaves being decussate, that is, in pairs one pair held at right angles to the next.

Ornamentally, this is a most attractive dwarf conifer with sprays of scale-like leaves borne one on top of another in broad feathery layers. No more than 50cm (21in) in height – eventually – it can spread to several metres (yards) forming a low, loose mound of leafy growth. The colour of the foliage, bright green in summer, changes to a purplish brown or bronze in winter except in heavy shade where it remains green. It is perfectly hardy and easy in most soil, acid or alkaline, and is an ideal plant for ground cover, even in shade.

This tree associates well with other low growing conifers, especially junipers and offers an excellent contrast to dwarf rhododendrons, heaths and heathers. A specimen in my garden planted as a youngster in the winter of 1983/84 is now 148cm (59in) across. It grows in an island bed on an acid sand with a dwarf Mexican mountain pine, *Pinus culminicola, Rhododendron yakushimanum* and several winter flowering heaths (*Erica carnea*). I find the contrasts of colour and form in this grouping very pleasing, though I suspect that if unchecked, the microbiota will eventually occupy the entire bed. A specimen at the Arboretum Trompenburg in Rotterdam, Holland reached 3.5m (12ft) across and no more than 20cm (8in) high in ten years.

Although it can be grown from seed when available, it is normally increased by nurserymen from cuttings. Commercially available only in the last ten years, it is now offered by an increasing number of sources.

Microbiota decussata – *the bright green summer foliage contrasts well with heathers. Boskoop, Holland (August).*

Picea breweriana

Picea breweriana – beautiful spindle-shaped young cones. Holly Cottage, Hampshire (August).

William Henry Brewer, after whom *Picea breweriana* is named, was a geologist and botanist who played a major role in the California State Geological Survey in the 1800s. He travelled widely in the wilds of California collecting many new plants in the process. None, however, can have afforded him as much pleasure and satisfaction as this beautiful conifer commonly referred to as Brewer's spruce and in California as Weeping Spruce. According to the records, Brewer first discovered his spruce in 1863 in the Siskiyou Mountains of northern California, and southern Oregon. The first living specimen in Britain was received at Kew Gardens in 1897, a gift from Professor Charles Sargent, Director of the Arnold Arboretum, Massachusetts.

It is one of three wild spruces with naturally weeping branchlets but neither of the others match it in total effect. In the wild, where it is now rare, it is confined to a few locations in deep ravines high in the mountains. Here it occasionally reaches as much as 35m (114ft) but is generally much less. In cultivation there are trees of 15 to 20m (50 to 65ft) while the majority are far smaller. It develops a straight stemmed, conical habit with a pointed crown, the branches sweeping outwards and upwards in the upper crown but downwards in the lower regions. From all branches the slender branchlets hang in long streamers which may be a metre (yard) or more long on a well established tree.

The green and grey lined, flattened, needle-like leaves point forward and are densely arranged all round the branchlets giving them a tail like effect, softer to the touch than is normally the case with spruces. On a flourishing tree, the branchlets are like luxurious curtains hanging from the branches and there is no more beautiful effect than an isolated specimen planted in a large lawn or on a grassy slope. Occasionally, one sees several Brewer's spruce planted as a group when the effect is stunning.

To the beauty of its habit one can add the bonus of its elegant drooping cones which are cigar shaped, 8 to 10cm (3 to 4in) long, green at first passing to purple and finally yellowish brown. It is amenable to a wide range of soils, acid or alkaline, so long as moisture is available. It also appreciates the shelter of other trees (not too close, however) but needs room in which to develop and be admired. Nurserymen increase this spruce either by grafting or from seed. Grafting produces an early effect but seedlings are preferable in the long term though they may be 15 years old before they develop the weeping effect. Indeed, when I worked for a nursery many years ago, we occasionally had seed-grown Brewer's spruce returned by customers who believed they had been sent the wrong plant. Unspectacular though they are when young, seedlings eventually 'come good' and older specimens are every bit as attractive as grafted trees. Hailing from the western mountains of the USA, it is not a happy tree in dry regions nor does it take kindly to inner city gardens especially if air pollution is present.

Opposite: Picea breweriana – *a young tree well clothed with weeping branchlets. Knightshayes Court, Devon (March).*

Pinus longaeva – *an ancient tree in the White Mountains of California (October).*

Pinus aristata

The headline in the local newspaper ran 'World's oldest living thing in a Shropshire garden'. Then followed a report telling how I had planted in my father-in-law's cottage garden, a young specimen of a Bristle-cone pine, *Pinus aristata* from the Rocky Mountains, Colorado, USA. Naturally it was pointed out that although the Shropshire specimen was itself only three years old, it had originated as seed from a tree nearer 3,000 years old.

P. aristata is one of a small group of closely related pines which grow in the wild in high mountains in south west United States and New

Mexico. Two of these species, *P. aristata* and *P. longaeva*, are referred to as bristlecone pines from the projecting bristle-like tips of the young cone scales. The name *aristata* meaning 'awned' refers to the same character. Because of the exposure and the low rainfall experienced by these mountains, the pines grow extremely slowly and when long past maturity cling tenaciously to life, resulting in trees of great age.

In 1985, I was taken up into the White Mountains of eastern California to see one of the bristlecone pines *P. longaeva*. At an altitude of around 3,650m (12,000ft) we found the pines often scattered in groves along the crest of the ridge. For some hours we wandered through the pines constantly stopping to admire their rugged beauty.

Pinus aristata – a densely branched young tree. The Hillier Arboretum, Hampshire (March).

Some specimens seemed to be no more than dead hulks bleached white by the sun but on closere examination they often supported one or more living branches with bunches of closely packed shining green needles. One grizzly old specimen had been given the name Alpha in recognition of its having been the first of these pines to be dated in excess of 4,000 years. Some distance away was another, even older specimen, nicknamed Methuselah claimed to be the world's 'Oldest Living Thing' at 4,680 years. The long lived nature of this pine is referred to in the name *longaeva*.

Although first introduced into cultivation as long ago as 1863, *P. aristata* remains uncommon outside of botanic gardens and specialist collections. While not in the front rank of ornamental pines its botanical and historical significance is deserving of a place in all but the smallest gardens. It is a hardy tree and although faster growing in cultivation than in its homeland, it is not one of the largest growing pines, the tallest recorded British specimen being a tree of 12m (38ft). The specimen in my late father-in-law's garden, by the way, is now 3m (9ft) after some ten years.

Pinus aristata is conical and densely branched in habit when young, the whorls of the branches becoming more open and spaced with age. The needles in bundles of five are spread evenly all around the shoots giving them a fox-tail like appearance. The needles are shining green and characteristically speckled with resin which turns white on drying. *Pinus longaeva* which has only been available in Britain over the last 15 years or so, differs mainly in the needles lacking the resin flecks. Either tree is suitable for specimen planting in a lawn or bed, associating well with heathers and other low growing shrubs. They are increased by nurserymen from seed, when available, or by grafting.

Pinus bungeana

'The more one sees of them, the more one loves them – in rain, bright sunshine, soft moonlight or snow laden, their exquisite appearance cannot fail to exert an uplifting influence on one's mind.' So wrote the Dutch American plant collector Frank Meyer about the Lacebark pine – *Pinus bungeana*. Meyer, on his extensive travels through north, east and central China in the first two decades of this century encountered the Lacebark pine on numerous occasions, both in the wild and in cultivation and anyone lucky enough to have seen it in its home country will perhaps understand his emotional response. Although it possesses an attractive and relatively light canopy for a pine, its main claim to fame rests on its beautiful bark.

On the stem and major branches the bark flakes away when old, rather like that of a plane tree or a buttonwood, producing an attractive marbling effect with greys, silvers, pale yellows and greens predominating. In China and other countries enjoying a continental climate – hot summers and cold winters – the bark effect is exceptional. In addition, the younger branches develop a milky white appearance which is not found on trees in British cultivation due to the generally wetter, cooler climate. This is not to say, of course, that the Lacebark pine is not worth growing on the contrary, its slow growth and compact habit, when young, makes it suitable even for small gardens, while its flaking bark is quite as colourful as it is in China even if it lacks the same degree of brilliance.

Pinus bungeana – *the beautiful dappled bark. Forbidden City, Beijing, China (May).*

The Lacebark is considered wild in several Chinese provinces but its extensive planting there over several centuries has blurred the true pattern of its native distribution. It is a tree with a long standing historical and religious significance and is commonly found planted in the vicinity of temples and monasteries. Not surprisingly, it was highly regarded by the Emperors who had it planted in the gardens and courtyards of their palaces where they could watch the play of light on its bark and admire the sun highlighting its glistening canopy. There are several large specimens of this pine in the Imperial Garden of the Forbidden City in Beijing (Peking) including one of 30m (100ft), or more, which must be many centuries old.

First collected in 1831 by a Russian, Alexander von Bunge, after whom it is named, *P. bungeana* was introduced to the west 15 years later by the Scot, Robert Fortune, one of the most successful of all 19th-century plant collectors. Over 100 years later, it is still uncommon in gardens, and is mainly found in Botanic gardens and other specialist collections. It is quite hardy and adaptable to most soils, except those badly drained. The largest specimen in British cultivation is a tree of 15.5m (50ft) in Kew Gardens, though it has taken many years to reach this size. It withstands drought tolerably well and is worth considering as a courtyard tree in city areas where it should benefit from reflected heat though it dislikes asmospheric pollution. It is not commonly available and when small plants are offered they have either been grown from imported seed or as a result of grafting.

Once established it makes an impressive lawn specimen with its open stemmed habit and spreading branches and associates well with buildings against which its marbled bark is a striking contrast.

Perennials and others

Actaea rubra

All those who have ever been on a wild flower hunt to the limestone areas of northern England will remember with special pleasure the plants which are particularly prevalent on the broad expanses of limestone paving in West Yorkshire and north Lancashire. The Columbine, Bloody Cranesbill and Angular Solomon's Seal are just a few of those I have seen over the years whilst another is the Baneberry—*Actaea spicata*. This is a member of the Buttercup family (*Ranunculaceae*) although at a glance bearing no obvious comparison. It is an undistinguished herb with much divided leaves and erect stems of 30 to 60cm (1 to 2ft) bearing racemes of fluffy white flowers in late spring. These are later followed by shining black, poisonous berries. It is not a common plant in Britain and even less so in gardens where its place is most often taken by the far more ornamental Red Baneberry, *Actaea rubra* of north-east American woodlands.

This, has astilbe-like foliage while the spikes of white flowers, quite attractive *en-masse*, are borne on slightly shorter stems up to 45cm

Opposite: Actaea rubra – *dense clusters of sealing-wax red berries. The Gables, Shropshire (July).*

(18in) on average. The main merit of this perennial lies in its berries which from a shining jade green, mature to sealing-wax red. They are carried in conspicuous dense terminal clusters from late summer into autumn. Although apparently less dangerous than those of the Common Baneberry, these fruits are nevertheless poisonous and should not be eaten. I would not recommend it to be planted without precautions in a garden where young children are likely to wander, but it is certainly worth considering for the woodland bed or shady border, especially with other woodlanders such as trilliums, epimediums and ferns. It is also worth planting among deciduous shrubs such as azaleas – evergreen and deciduous.

Hardy and easy in sun or shade on any ordinary moisture-retentive soil, it expands slowly to eventually make a sizeable clump. The name *rubra* describes the colour of the berries. Although division is possible, nurserymen generally increase this plant from seed.

Allium cernuum

As a boy, I believed that the only onions were those cultivated with loving care on the vegetable plots in the allotments around my home town. Then I developed an interest in wild flowers and pursuing this with great enthusiasm, I tramped in all the wild places within a ten mile radius of the town hall. One day in spring, I found myself in an unfamiliar wood through which snaked a small stream. As I progressed through the trees I found myself walking through a continuous ground cover of large fleshy, plantain-like leaves above which rose three cornered stems bearing clusters of starry white flowers. Although I did not realize it at the time, it was my first encounter with Britain's native Ransoms or Wild Garlic, *Allium ursinum*, whose pungent smell soon assailed my nose. It was the beginning of a fascination for ornamental onions which led me to collect the more ornamental kinds in my gardens, carrying some with me whenever I moved home.

In my present garden on an acid sand, I grow some 15 different kinds and this is merely the tip of the iceberg for there are hundreds all told, many of which are eminently suited to cultivation. In general, they are an easy and hardy group of bulbous plants most of them requiring nothing more than full sun and an ordinary garden soil. Good drainage is a bonus but not a prerequisite of survival for many of those commonly available and this includes *A. cernuum*, the Nodding Onion from North America. In the wild, it is widespread and variable in form depending on habitat, but all are immediately recognizable by their drooping terminal flower heads, rising above tufts of narrow flattened, slightly grey-green leaves.

Graham Thomas has described the flower head as resembling an exploding rocket and as usual he has it just right. He is also responsible for distributing a lovely rich amethyst form of this onion which was originally grown by John Wall, a former curator of Wisley Garden. This is the plant I grow and there is none finer in my opinion, an established clump putting up numerous stems up to 45cm (18in). The terminal portion bends over like a shepherd's crook before 'exploding' a shower of drooping bell-shaped flowers, each with a protruding tongue of whitish stamens. The flowers often begin in early summer and are at their best in late summer.

In the wild, its flowers range in colour from pale pink to rose, purple

Opposite: Allium cernum –
flower-heads like exploding rockets.
Author's garden, Hampshire (August).

or white and one must beware of inferior forms with 'wishy washy' flowers The name *cernuum* means 'nodding' or 'drooping' which aptly describes the flowers of this onion. With age, however, they become erect and once the seed has been shed or gathered, make charming additions to dried arrangements in the home. *A. cernuum* is easily grown from seed or bulbs which should be planted to 12.5cm (5in) deep in autumn.

Anemonella thalictroides 'Schoaff's Double'

Anemonella thalictroides is one of those plants whose botanical status botanists have argued about for years. It is a diminutive member of the buttercup family (*Ranunculaceae*) with a distinct affinity to the anemones. Indeed, the present name *Anemonella* is a diminutive of *Anemone*, literally 'small anemone'. Its descriptive name *thalictroides*, however, refers to its likeness to a *Thalictrum* species. In fact, since it first became known to the botanical world, it has been known under several different names, viz. *Anemone thalictroides*, *Thalictrum anemonoides*, *Syndesmon thalictroides* and currently *Anemonella thalictroides*.

By contrast, gardeners are in no doubt whatsoever as to the ornamental merits of this plant which has been known in cultivation for a very long time. It is a charming little spring-flowering woodlander, native to eastern North America. From a tuberous rootstock, the smooth slender stems rise to 15 or 18cm (6 or 8in), usually bearing at their summits three slender-stalked, white or pale pink six-petalled flowers, up to 2.5cm (1in) across. The leaves are borne in a ring around the stem and are divided into three to six rounded three-lobed leaflets. It is a hardy perennial requiring a shady, moist, but well-drained, soil given which it will quietly expand to form small patches.

Over the years there have been several double-flowered forms in cultivation, usually under the name 'Flore Pleno'. In late April 1985, I had the pleasure of visiting Harold Epstein at his home near New York. Harold is well known as a plant collector and his garden is a treasury of choice and little known plants, most of which thrive in woodland beds. Among the many flowering perennials which caught my eye that day was an exquisite form of *Anemonella thalictroides* known as 'Schoaff's Double'. Quite who Schoaff was I did not ascertain but his anemonella is a little gem. The six petals (correctly sepals) of the flower are topped by layer upon layer of smaller narrower petals to form a neatly crowded pale pink head with the clustered carpets forming a small green heart. It was planted in several parts of the garden forming low colonies.

It is well known that double flowered forms are not necessarily an improvement on the typical flower but there is no doubt in my mind as to the merit of 'Schoaff's Double'. It is increased by carefully detaching rooted pieces from the periphery of the colony while typical *A. thalictroides* may also be raised from seed. To my knowledge, it is not yet commercially available in Britain but I make no excuses for including it here, in the hope that some skilled and enterprising nurseryman will soon rectify the situation.

Arisaema sikokianum

My first sight of the native Cuckoo Pint *Arum maculatum* was on a woodland margin within sight of Pendle Hill, legendary home of the Lancashire witches. There were hundreds of plants crowding a shady bank, their pale green spathes slightly parted to reveal a purplish, poker-like spadix, hence the alternative names of Priest in the Pulpit or Jack in the Pulpit. The spadix carries towards its base the reproductive organs which are protected by the sheathing base of the spathe.

Anemonella thalictroides *'Schoaff's Double' – a choice little woodlander. La Rochelle, New York (April).*

Arisaema sikokianum. *Above: a fine colony in a woodland garden. La Rochelle, New York (April). Below: the striking white throat and spadix. La Rochelle, New York (April).*

Since that day, I have seen many other members of the arum family (aroids) in places as far afield as North America, Greece and China. They are a greatly varied throng sometimes beautiful, sometimes bizzare but always striking in flower. Asia is home to a large number of aroids among which the arisaemas provide us with some of the hardiest and most satisfactory for garden purposes. Among these, *Arisaema sikokianum* is, without doubt, one of the most distinct and desirable.

An exotic relative of the American native Jack in the Pulpit (*A. triphyllum*), it grows like most of its kin from a corm or tuber. First to appear are a number of erect sheathing bracts which are attractively marbled followed by two long-stalked leaves with tightly folded sheathing bases, together forming a false stem of pseudostem. The solitary flower emerges from the upper leaf sheath and consists of a spathe and spadix, the former funnel-shaped in its lower half expanding into a sail-like, long-pointed limb above. In colour the spathe is dark purple or brownish purple on the outside marked with pale stripes while the inside of the limb is greenish with greenish-white stripes. The throat is milky white from which rises the purple based spadix expanding to form a white bulbous head at its summit. The effect is dramatic, especially so when a group of plants are flowering together. Not surprisingly, this species was once known as *A. magnificum*.

The two long-stalked leaves with a sheathing base are arranged one above the other on the stem. The leaf blade is composed of three to five pointed leaflets, toothed or entire at the margins. The flowers may begin opening as early as spring but are normally at their best in early summer. It is a native of woodlands in south Japan and was introduced to western cultivation in 1938. It is a hardy and robust species up to

45cm (18in), depending on maturity and growing conditions, and flourishes in a cool moist, but well-drained leafy soil, preferably with light or dappled shade. It does not enjoy dry soils or waterlogged conditions and early emerging shoots may need to be given the temporary protection of a pane of glass or a clear plastic cover.

Out of doors in the west it is perhaps best grown in warmer southern areas whilst in colder areas it may be grown in deep pots in a cool greenhouse or cold frame. Tubers should be planted 10 to 12.5cm (4 to 5in) deep with a little coarse sand or grit beneath them to help prevent rotting should wet conditions prevail. The finest display I ever saw was in the woodland garden of Harold Epstein near New York in late April 1985. Among many lovely and impressive flowering plants growing there it was the most strikingly beautiful and obviously very happy in the leafy soil. Although naturally enjoying hot dry summers, the moisture level of Harold Epstein's soil is maintained by overhead sprays attached to the stems of trees.

Arisaema sikokianum is increased from seed, when available, or from young tubers.

Ballota pseudodictamnus

Several years ago, I had the opportunity to visit the island of Crete. The largest of the Aegean islands, it is a paradise for plant lovers. While spring is the most favoured time because of the wealth of early flowers, so rich is the flora that a visit at any time will reward the diligent with a sight of plants fascinating as well as colourful.

Inland from the capital Iraklion, is an isolated limestone mountain from the top of which one can obtain a magnificent view of olive

Ballota acetabulosa – *grey perennial with conspicuous woolly calyces. The Meteora, Greece (June).*

groves and vineyards in the valleys below. The pale limestone cliffs and the rocky slopes below support a wealth of small shrubs and perennials that revel in the sun and the hot dry conditions of summer. One of these perennials is *Ballota pseudodictamnus*, the 'False Dittany' which makes a low mound of woolly grey growth sometimes difficult to see against the limestone. The mounds can be as much as 60cm (2ft) high by 1m (3ft) across, the stems like the foliage, covered with a dense grey pelt of woolly hairs which is soft to the touch, like a lamb's ear.

The flowers are borne in distant whorls from the axils of the paired rounded leaves in summer and are of little ornamental merit being quite small, two lipped and white with purplish spots. They arise from small funnel shaped calyces which develop into small, furry umbrella shaped seed vessels after flowering. It is a most attractive perennial of its kind and one which has earned for itself a popular and permanent place in our gardens.

The name *pseudodictamnus*, meaning 'False Dittany', derives from the Greek *pseudo* (false) and *Dictamnus* – the Greek name for the Cretan Dittany (*Origanum dictamnus*) to which this ballota bears a superficial resemblance. It lacks, however, the medicinal attributes of *O. dictamnus*.

Closely related is *Ballota acetabulosa*, also native to Greece and Crete. Like the other, it makes a low bushy plant with densely grey woolly stems but the leaves lack the slight yellowish cast characteristic of *B. pseudodictamnus*. It differs too, in the closer whorls of flowers, the calyces of which enlarge to 1.5 to 2cm ($\frac{1}{2}$ to $\frac{3}{4}$in) across after flowering, forming conspicuous congested spikes of pale greenish-grey, saucer shaped seed vessels, hence the name *acetabulosa*, meaning saucer shaped. The seed vessels were once used by country people as floating wicks in olive oil lamps, which is why the Greeks call this plant 'Louminia'. Although the above story may sound a little far-fetched I can confirm that it actually works. In the absence of *B. acetabulosa* I have used the smaller seed vessels of *B. pseudodictamnus*. One simply pours a film of olive oil in a saucer and then floats the seed vessels, pointed ends up, until they have soaked up sufficient of the oil to burn when touched with a lighted match. Several wicks give just enough light to read by.

What I recommend for these two ballotas is a sunny, well drained site in the garden where they provide an effective contrast to green and purple-leaved plants, especially the purple-leaved sedums. They blend particularly well with stone and red brick and are ideal when established in cracks or small beds in paved areas such as patios and they thrive in rubble soils. Considering their liking for sun and heat, they are remarkably adaptable to our cool temperate climate though they do not always survive winters nor do they care for winter wet. More often than not, severe frost will kill them hard back but if the limp growths are cut clean away in spring the plant will often sprout anew from the base. Winter protection, such as a pane of glass, or cloche, is preferable to a polythene or plastic cover which may cause sweating and subsequent decay. Both these ballotas are normally increased by nurserymen from cuttings.

Ballota pseudodictamnus – *ideal for sunny terraces and paved areas. Mount Stewart, N. Ireland (July).*

Bletilla striata

The first time I met with *Bletilla striata* was on a June visit to Kew Gardens some years ago. It was flourishing in a sunny border at the base of a wall and flowering its heart out. I thought it one of the most beautiful flowers I had ever seen and there and then resolved to grow it in my own garden one day. I did not have a garden at the time and it was several years before I did but as soon as I moved into the present house in south Hampshire, I began my search for the bletilla. I found it being offered by a specialist nurseryman and planted it in a west-facing border beneath my study window where it soon settled in. That was four years ago and last year it produced just three flowering stems, a long way off Kew's display but good enough for starters.

Bletilla striata, sometimes catalogued under the name *B. hyacinthina*, is a terrestrial orchid from grassy hillsides in China and Japan which, despite its rather exotic appearance when in flower, is relatively easy to grow and is hardy in cultivation. It is herbaceous in nature, the cane-like shoots rising from a string of pseudobulbs to a height of about 40cm (16in). There are normally several shoots per plant each bearing several boldly ribbed or pleated, arching, sword-shaped green leaves 45 to 60cm (18 to 24in) long. These alone are worth growing this plant for, having the aspect of a handsome dwarf bamboo.

The flowers are borne on slender shoots well clear of the leaves, five to ten flowers per shoot, opening in succession from late spring through to early summer. Individually they are shaped not unlike those of the famous Cattleya orchid, 4 to 5cm (1½ to 2in) across, rose lavender in colour except for the end of the lip which is deep rose-purple. Inside the lower surface of the lip are several white-frilled ridges or ribs adding further to the beauty of the flower. A lovely white form of this species, forma *gebina*, is occasionally available and should be snapped up immediately if seen. I have heard of some gardeners who grow this orchid in a cool leafy soil in partial shade, that it has proved relatively shy flowering. In my experience it flowers best in a sunny situation and a well-drained soil. Indeed, surprisingly for an orchid in cultivation, it seems relatively unfussed as to soil as long as it is not wet or a heavy clay. I once saw a close relative of this species – *B. ochracea*, growing wild on the steep sandy banks of a stream in central China where it revelled in the sun, despite the occasional trampling by water buffalo.

On a visit to the lakes region of northern Italy in 1986, I saw *Bletilla striata* flourishing there in several gardens, including the extraordinary Isola Bella in Lake Maggiore where a whole border was filled with this plant, its flowers creating a rich purple band at the base of a sunny wall. The soil in this border was poor and stony with little if any organic content. Some growers of *bletilla* find that a liquid feed of manure water, or similar, when the plant is in active growth considerably improves performance. Another successful American grower adds a mulch or top dressing of pine needles to his *bletilla* bed each year.

It is normally increased by nurserymen by careful division of the pseudobulbs and first time growers are best advised to try established plants in pots. If tubers are purchased, these should be planted 5 to 7.5cm (2 to 3in) deep. Winter protection is not normally necessary though in cold areas it might be prudent to cover the ground above the tubers with peat, pine needles, or some other temporary protection.

First introduced to Britain in 1802, its distribution in the wild is

Bletilla striata – *a most beautiful hardy ground orchid. Isola Bella, Italy (June).*

rather obscure due to its having been long cultivated both for its flowers and for its pseudobulbs which are used by the Chinese for medicinal purposes. The descriptive name *striata* refers to the ribbed leaves.

Carex elata 'Bowles' Golden'

The sedges – *Carex* species – are a large group of perennials with narrow grass-like leaves and characteristic three-cornered, flowering shoots. The flowers are individually quite small and in most species densely packed into spikes or spikelets towards the summit of the shoot. Comparatively few are colourful enough in flower to be considered for

the garden though some are attractive in the way the spikelets are carried. An example of this is *Carex pendula*, the Pendulous Sedge, whose long drooping spikelets are borne along tall arching shoots. Other sedges are worth growing for their bold clumps of leaves which in some selections are coloured or striped.

Arguably, the best of the coloured leaved sedges is *Carex elata* 'Bowles' Golden' sometimes incorrectly referred to as *C. stricta* 'Aurea'. The typical green plant known as the Tufted Sedge, is a British native being found by rivers, lakes and in fens. It is also an important member of East Anglian reed-swamps. It is mainly found in eastern England and central Ireland where base rich fens are common. It is in Cambridge-shire, at Wicken Fen that E. A. Bowles, the famous plantsman and gardener found his golden form while hunting for moths. It forms a

large dense clump of up to 76cm (30in) with narrow arching and drooping leaves which, in a position open to the sun, are a brilliant golden-yellow with the thinnest of green margins. The display begins in late spring continuing until the end of summer when the approaching autumn brings it to a quiet finale.

There is a completely golden selection of 'Bowles' Golden' incidentally, known as 'Knightshayes' after the Devon garden in which it was raised. 'Bowles' Golden' needs a moist soil in which to thrive and even then it can be frustratingly slow or even unwilling to establish. For the most impressive effects it should be planted in groups or, given the space, in drifts on the margins of pools where it will create bold bright bands the summer through. The ideal position appears to be one in which the roots have ready access to water but the crown is not subject to regular or long term flooding. A bed or border alongside the pool margin is the best answer.

It is important that the planting position is not overshadowed by trees as the leaves will not colour up in shade. The finest planting I have seen of 'Bowles' Golden' is on the margins of pools in the Water Garden at Longstock Park near Stockbridge in Hampshire. The gardens are situated on a peat deposit in an otherwise chalk valley with perhaps the most famous chalk river of all, the Test, passing nearby. It could well be that the water in the pools is sufficiently alkaline to remind the sedge of its base – rich native fens. The name *elata*, meaning tall, presumably refers to the flowering shoots which, however, are no taller than average and less than those of several other native sedges.

C. elata 'Bowles' Golden' is increased by nurserymen from division but the results are by no means as successful as one might expect which explains in part why this sedge is not as commonly seen as its merit deserves.

Chusquea couleou

Although sometimes classed with shrubs, the bamboos are no more than woody stemmed grasses and for the purposes of this book are treated as perennials. Out of the numerous hardy bamboos at present grown in cultivation, *Chusquea couleou* is one of the most distinct and easily recognized. Its dense clumps of stiffly erect canes set it apart from others in a collection and mark it out as a bamboo worthy of planting as a specimen in a lawn or border. Like others of its clan, it is evergreen so its effect can be appreciated throughout the year, especially when planted in isolation away from other evergreens.

It is native to the Andes of Chile and Argentina from whence it was first introduced to the west as seed by Harold Comber in 1926 and again 13 years later from the Magellan region by L. Bridges. Botanically, it is easily distinguished from other bamboos in general cultivation by its canes which are solid between the nodes (joints) rather than hollow. New canes from established clumps can grow as much as 5.5m (18ft) in their first year (even taller in the wild) though on young plants the canes are more often less than 5m (16ft). A deep olive green in colour, they are partially clothed with white papery, close-fitting sheaths which give the canes an attractive bi-coloured effect. The following year, from the node beneath each sheath, springs a bunch of slender branches which grow up to 45cm (18in) long, bearing narrow, slender-pointed, deep green leaves up to 7cm (2½in) long. The branches

Carex elata 'Bowles' Golden' – one of the best golden leaved plants for waterside. Longstock Water Garden, Hampshire (August).

almost encircle the cane and occur at regular intervals giving the cane a 'fox-tail' effect which is as attractive as it is characteristic. The canes mature from green in the early years to a dull yellowish shade.

Unlike many bamboos in cultivation of Asiatic origin, *Chusquea couleou* has not been known to flower. Although mainly found in climatically mild gardens, it appears to be fairly hardy and is equally adaptable to drought though it is not recommended for dry soils. Some specimens in colder inland gardens have been damaged during recent severe winters but these have generally sprouted anew the following year. It enjoys a reasonably fertile, well-drained soil, acid or alkaline and looks well when planted by water as long as its roots are not subject to flooding.

It is increased (though slowly) by nurserymen from division. Like all bamboos, *Chusquea couleou* is a gross feeder and established clumps respond well to annual top dressing with a quick-acting fertilizer in spring. They do not object to an occasional mulching with compost, leaf mould or well rotted manure. The name *couleou*, by the way, is derived from the native Chilean name for this bamboo.

Opposite: Chusquea couleou – *a bold bamboo with densely leafy canes. Burford House, Worcestershire (April).*

Crinum × powellii

The crinums are a group of 100 or so bulbous perennials from the tropics and subtropics where they are often found on sea coasts. The majority are too tender for cultivation out of doors in the British Isles but *Crinum longifolium* and *C. moorei*, both from southern Africa, are sometimes grown in gardens in warmer districts. A hybrid between these two *C. × powellii*, however, is the most commonly cultivated crinum and there are few more lovely flowers.

Crinum × powellii – *bold clumps flanking a path. Jenkyn Place, Hampshire (August).*

C. × powelli is a garden hybrid raised in about 1885 by C. Baden-Powell, inheriting the relative hardiness of *C. longifolium* (better known as *C. bulbispermum*) and the flower quality of *C. moorei*. The large flask-shaped bulb up to 20cm (8in) across, has a long neck which rises clear of the soil surface. In spring it produces long fleshy, strap-shaped green leaves which collectively form large lush clumps, or piles. During the summer flowers rise above these, carried in loose terminal umbels on stout stems up to 1.2m (4ft). The individual flowers are trumpet-shaped, rose-pink and sweetly fragrant. They are borne continuously over a period of several weeks, new flowers opening as earlier ones fade. There are several named selections including 'Album', 'Haarle-mense' and 'Krelagei' with flowers of white, pale pink and deep pink respectively. All are superior to the typical form.

Not surprisingly, considering the origin of its parents, *C. × powellii* revels in a warm sunny situation. It enjoys a fertile, moist but well-drained soil and normally flowers exceptionally well in a border or bed at the base of a sunny south-facing wall. In a Hampshire garden I know, *C. × powellii* has flourished for many years in a pair of borders flanking a brick path. Here, beneath old apple trees they regularly produce an abundance of flowers in late summer.

If it has one weakness, it is the untidy habit of the leaves once flowering is over but this is worth tolerating for its performance when in flower. It is increased by division of the clumps of bulbs which can be a tough and time-consuming operation. New bulbs should be planted with the tops of their necks above ground.

Dictamnus albus *var.* purpureus.
Above: a long lived perennial, handsome in flower. Kiftsgate Court, Gloucestershire (June). Opposite: individual flowers, orchid-like. The Hillier Arboretum, Hampshire (June).

Dictamnus albus var. *purpureus*

Some years ago, while leading a June flower tour to Greece, I stopped our coach one day to demonstrate to the party a piece of 'magic' concerning a wild plant growing on the roadside. It was one of those lovely hot days for which Greece is famous and as I scrambled out of the coach to pick a flowering spike of the plant, our driver and guide (both Greeks) watched me with interest. They were even more curious when, on regaining the coach I asked if I could borrow the driver's cigarette lighter. Holding the flower spike upright in one hand I placed the lighter close to its base and flicked the wheel to spark it. The gas ignited and a blue flame raced through the spike to its summit, a distance of some 30 to 35cm (12 to 14in), leaving the flowers unharmed and unblemished.

Members of the party unfamiliar with the Burning Bush or Gas Plant *Dictamnus albus* were delighted by my party trick but their pleasure was nothing compared with the looks of amazement on the faces of our driver and guide. They just could not understand how this demonstration had been achieved. Even after a careful explanation followed by a repeat performance with another flowering spike they continued to shake their heads in disbelief exclaiming 'incredible' or whatever Greek's say when puzzled and impressed!

The explanation is simple when one examines the flowering spikes closely for they are covered with tiny, shining wart-like glands which exude a volatile oil or gas. The glands cover the main flowering stem and flower stalks but are especially thick on the developing fruits. Just the right conditions of calm and warmth are needed to persuade the gas to ignite and attempts to demonstrate this trick in cool temperate

gardens have varied results. A warm, calm, sultry evening offers the best chance.

Flames and tricks apart though, *Dictamnus albus* is a handsome and desirable perennial for the garden and one I would never be without. It is a pity that young plants are slow to establish and due to their late emergence in the year are easily damaged or killed as a result of an accident with hoe, spade or boot. It is one of these plants whose position in the border needs to be clearly marked with a stout label or a small cane. It is a long-lived plant developing with age a woody base from which the erect stems up to 1m (3ft) arise, the upper half or third bearing long-stalked, five-petalled flowers reminiscent of an orchid or a bauhinia in effect. The flower colour varies from white in typical *D. albus* to a pale mauve-purple with darker veins in the variety *purpureus*. These open in succession from the base upwards during early summer and if a single spike is beautiful, then an established clump in flower can be regarded as a show-stopper. Although I refer to the flowers being borne in a spike they are in fact carried in racemes, the invidual flowers carried on stalks along the main axis.

The leaves are deeply divided giving off an aroma of lemon peel when gently rubbed which is not surprising considering that it belongs to the rue family (*Rutaceae*) of which most members, if not all, are pungently aromatic. It is found in the wild over a wide area of Europe and Asia where it favours rocky hillsides or stony slopes in sun or partial shade.

It is hardy in cool temperate zones performing best in a sunny position and a fertile, well-drained soil, acid or alkaline. It can be increased from seed or by careful division though in my experience, established plants are best left alone and resent being dug up. Seed grown plants in pots are normally offered by nurserymen and this is the best way of starting. The ripe seed pods explode if left drying in a warm room and are best contained in a paper bag. The names *albus* (white) and *pupureus* (purple) are self explanatory while the alternative, if now incorrect, name *D. fraxinella*, meaning 'small *Fraxinus*' refers to the leaves which are pinnately divided like those of an ash.

Dryopteris wallichiana

One of the most widespread plants in the world's wild places is a fern — the common Bracken, *Pteridium aquilinum*. Apart from Europe, I have seen it on my travels in China, the Himalaya, North America and down under in New Zealand. It is said to occur in all five continents and when one considers how quickly it spreads and the large areas of moor and heath it covers in Britain alone, its worldwide dominance is perhaps not so surprising. No-one in their right mind would wish to introduce plants of Bracken into the garden but there are a large number of other ferns that are well worth considering, one of which is *Dryopteris wallichiana*.

The descriptive name commemorates Dr. Nathaniel Wallich, who from 1815–41 was Superintendent of the Calcutta Botanic garden assisting numerous botanists and plant collectors arriving in Calcutta on their way to the forests and mountains of northern India. *D. wallichiana* is common in the Himalaya and if recent botanical opinion is to be followed this fern is also represented in China, Japan, south and central America, Hawaii, Zimbabwe, Tristan da Cunha and Madagascar.

Opposite: Dryopteris wallichiana — a bold fern with golden scaly stalks. Author's garden, Hampshire (July).

Opposite: Dryopteris wallichiana – *a bold fern with golden scaly stalks. Author's garden, Hampshire (July).*

It is a handsome, hardy fern forming a big bold clump – like a shuttlecock in form with lance-shaped fronds up to 1.5m (5ft) tall. Even in spring, they are beautiful and fascinating to observe, rising from the dense scaly rhizome like bishops' croziers clothed with shining blackish or reddish-brown pointed scales. The fern frond is composed of three main parts, the basal stalk, called the stipe which becomes the rachis as it continues upward. Attached to the rachis are leafy segments (pinnae) which collectively make up the blade of the frond. In *D. wallichiana*, the stipe and rachis are covered, like the rhizome, with a rich coat of dark shining scales which are particularly attractive when highlighted by the sun. The blade is rather leathery in texture, deeply cut and of a bright shining green, a perfect contrast to the rachis.

Although I grew *D. wallichiana* with reasonable success on a dry chalk soil in my previous garden, it increased in stature and effectiveness when moved to a moist loam in shade. It is not averse to lime in the soil as long as there is sufficient moisture available in summer while the provision of some shade helps encourage the production of taller fronds. Whether it is used alone as a spot plant or in bold group, *D. wallichiana* is an outstanding fern which deserves to be seen far more than at present. It is especially effective when associated with candelabra primulas and meconopsis and is just as attractive planted with hostas and other perennial plants with bold, broad foliage. It is increased by nurserymen from spores as well as by division.

Epimedium acuminatum

Mount Omei in China's Sichuan province, is one of the most if not *the* most famous mountains in botanical history. It is by no means a high mountain by Chinese standards, just over 3,000m (10,000ft), and yet it supports a rich flora with over 3,000 different kinds of plants. Ever since the plant hunter E. H. ('Chinese') Wilson first visited this mountain in the early part of this century and made known to western gardeners some of its more desirable treasures, Mount Omei has been regarded as a Mecca by plant enthusiasts. In 1980, I realized a long held ambition when I climbed the mountain for the first time and several plants grown from seeds collected at the time are now in cultivation. One of these is *Epimedium acuminatum*.

I am not aware that this plant was previously in cultivation but it is now being grown by several specialist nurserymen and should gradually become more available to gardeners as time goes by. It is a distinct epimedium in every way, developing bold clumps and patches up to 60cm (2ft) tall in time and in ideal conditions. The leaves have large, lance-shaped, slender-pointed leaflets, shining dark green above and a contrasting blue-green below. The descriptive name *acuminatum*, meaning 'tapering to a long slender point', refers to these leaflets. Handsome in leaf, *E. acuminatum* is among the longest flowering of all epimediums and, for that matter, one of the largest flowered.

The first flowers, carried on slender branching stems, appear just

Epimedium acuminatum – attractive bicoloured, long-spurred flowers. Author's garden, Hampshire (June).

clear of the leaves in mid spring to be followed by others through early summer. They measure 4 to 5cm. (1½ to 2in) across, with four long curving spurs and are a contrasting plum purple and white in colour, hanging on a delicate thread-like stalk. Like others of its clan, *E. acuminatum* is easy to grow on most soils, acid or alkaline, though ill-drained soils are best avoided. Light shade is appreciated which is not surprising considering its woodland home. It can be increased by seed or careful division.

Eryngium giganteum

Headbourne Worthy is a pretty little hamlet in the chalk country north of Winchester in Hampshire. Its main claim to garden fame is that Headbourne Worthy Grange was for many years the home of the Hon. Lewis Palmer (1894–1971), one time Treasurer of the Royal Horticultural Society and a keen plantsman and gardner. His plant interests were many and including South African bulbs among which watsonias and agapanthus were special favourites of his. It was as a result of numerous crosses between the species and varieties of agapanthus that Palmer provided the gardening world with a relatively hardy race of seedlings which came to be known as the Headbourne Hybrids.

I remember him showing me the parents of these hybrids on a visit to his garden in the 1960s. I also saw there many other interesting plants including *Eryingium giganteum* which, despite its descriptive name, is far from being the giant of its clan. I had been invited to visit Lewis Palmer on a weekday evening after work and I was excited by the prospect of meeting him for the first time and of seeing his famous plant collection. It was a marvellous warm summer evening and the sun was below the horizon when the tour ended with refreshments in his study. While standing in this room, drink in hand, I happened to glance through a window into the fast darkening garden. It was then that I saw the eryngium, a group of about half a dozen plants 1m (3ft) tall, growing in a border on the far side of a lawn. I did not know the identity of these plants but I was immediately struck by their almost luminous presence. They stood out in the gloom like some ghostly throng and confirmation of this was provided by Lewis Palmer when, in answer to my question, he told me that it was a selection of *Eryngium giganteum* known as Miss Willmott's Ghost.

The story behind this name has been told many times but is well worth repeating. First, let me describe the plant. *Eryngium giganteum* is a biennial member of a group of plants distributed in the wild through the temperate and sub-tropical regions. It includes two members of the British native flora in the Field Eryngio, *E. campestre*, and the Sea Holly, *E. maritum*. From seed, *E. giganteum* develops a bold rosette of long-stalked, heart-shaped, leathery, green, toothed leaves. Leaves are also borne on the stems but these are stalkless, deeply lobed and spine-toothed. The erect branching stems up to 1.2m (4ft) tall are produced during the second or third year, bearing at their extremities, dense, teasel like heads of tiny, pale blue or bluish-white flowers. Beneath each head is a ring of conspicuous broad-based, spine-toothed, leaf-like bracts. The flowers usually open from mid- to late summer, the terminal heads opening first, followed by the subsidiary ones. The entire plant has a rather stiff, leathery, spiny attraction which is considerably emphasized by the silvery-white bloom coating the

Eryngium giganteum – *ghostly stems and leaves. Powis Castle, Wales (September).*

leaves, bracts and stems. In the wild, *E. giganteum* sometimes has blue tinted bracts but those of the commonly cultivated plant are decidedly silvery. It is the latter characteristic which gave rise to the common name Miss Willmott's Ghost.

One story has it that *Eryngium giganteum* was a favourite of that great gardener Miss Ellen Willmott in her garden at Warley Place in Essex and naturally, she gave seed of this plant to her numerous gardening friends. Although biennial, it seeds itself around and plants are apt to spring up in the most unlikely places, often some distance away from the original planting position. After Miss Willmott's death in 1934, those in whose garden her eryngium was established were reminded of her generosity by the annual appearance of these ghostly seedlings.

Another version suggests that when visiting gardens Miss Willmott used to drop surreptitiously a few seeds of this plant here and there to surprise the owners in due course with its unexpected appearance.

A native of the Caucasus Mountains in south-east Russia, *E. giganteum* was first introduced into western cultivation as long ago as 1820 though it is still not as commonly grown as one would have expected. It is perfectly hardy and should be given a position in full sun or light shade in a well-drained, fertile soil. Having said that, it is remarkably adaptable and I have seen it thriving in a wide range of situations from chalky rubble to acid sand and once or twice in a vegetable plot where its singular appearance was considerably enhanced by the attendant potatoes and carrots. It can be grown with other perennials in herbaceous borders or beds or even among shrubs, but I believe that it should not be too crowded otherwise its poise and striking effect will be impaired. Self-sown seedlings are another matter and in those gardens where this plant is thoroughly at home, it can become something of a weed though the seedlings are easily disposed of with the hoe.

It is increased by seed which may be sown in pots or in situ. Nurserymen usually sell one-year-old plants which can be planted as soon as they become available.

Erysimum 'Bowles' Mauve'

Often referred to as perennial wallflowers, the erysimums also contain a number of annual, as well as biennial, members which are occasionally seen in cultivation though are by no means common. *Erysimum* 'Bowles' Mauve' is an evergreen subshrub and something of a mystery as no one seems certain of its origin. The name suggests that it was grown by E. A. Bowles in his garden at Myddelton House in Enfield but according to Mrs Frances Perry, who was a long time friend of Bowles, he never knew this plant.

It possesses certain characteristics of *E. linifoliium*, a native of Spain, and may be a hybrid of this species but there are other species from south-west Europe and the Canary isles which are just as likely to have been involved. Whatever its beginnings, there can be no doubting its ornamental merit although, like others of its kind, it is not long lived nor for that matter is it reliably hardy, except in milder areas. It soon makes a compact mound 30 to 60cm (1 to 2ft) high of sturdy branches clothed in their upper parts with long narrow, grey-green leaves. These are topped by long terminal racemes of mauve-purple, four-petalled flowers, darker in bud which open from the base upwards as the raceme elongates. The best display is in spring when the whole bush is in flower but flowers are produced off and on most other times of the year even in winter if the weather is mild.

It requires a warm, sunny position and is happy in most soils from acid to alkaline as long as it is well drained. One of the most obvious sites for this wallflower is the top of a dry wall or in a border at its base. It is probably longer lived when grown 'hard' than when it is given a too rich soil which encourages soft growth. Like rock roses (*Cistus* species) 'Bowles' Mauve' seems more able to tolerate cold conditions as a young plant. Old specimens are often killed during periods of severe weather, hence the prudence of having a young replacement ready to take its place. It is increased by nurserymen from cuttings.

Opposite: Erysimum *'Bowles' Mauve'* – a free flowering perennial for a sunny terrace or patio. Borde Hill Gardens, Sussex (April).

Euphorbia wallichii

In the Alpine pastures above Gulmarg in the Vale of Kashmir grows *Euphorbia wallichii*, one of the most striking and desirable of all herbaceous perennials for the garden. It is, of course, found elsewhere in that mountain kingdom and occurs more widely beyond its borders along the Himalaya from Afghanistan eastwards to China. Above Gulmarg however, it dominates the high plateaux in early summer, forming in some places a green and gold cloak for as far as the eye can see. It flourishes here despite the attentions of the ubiquitous goat and other grazing animals who each spring, following the receding snow,

Euphorbia wallichii – *the real McCoy! in the wild above Gulmarg in Kashmir (July).*

climb the steep slopes devouring all before them. The euphorbia survives the onslaught because of the caustic nature of its milk-white juice, a feature it shares with all other members of its family.

Like so many high mountain plants, it starts into growth as soon as the snow departs, sometimes before, and a period of furious activity results in a bold clump or mound of leafy shoots up to 60cm (2ft) tall by 1m (3ft) across. The leaves are 8.75 to 13cm (3 to 5in) long tapering to a point and carry a pale midrib, a characteristic of several other ornamental euphorbias. The uppermost leaves or bracts are slightly smaller and yellow or yellowish green forming a loose ruff beneath each flower head. The flowers themselves, as in most other euphorbias, are comparatively small and insignificant but they are made conspicuous by the yellow cups in which they are set and the yellow bracts beneath. Seen against the rich green of the foliage, the flower heads appear as bright golden stars.

In cultivation, *E. wallichii* seems to have had a chequered career. The date of its first introduction appears to have been unrecorded although it is likely to have occurred during the first half of the last century. It was named after Dr. Nathaniel Wallich, from 1814 to 1841 Director of the Calcutta Botanic Garden, a plant collector of note who is specially remembered for the help he gave other collectors visiting India. It appears never to have been common in cultivation and even now its exact status is confused by the number of imposters which are grown under this name. While these are ornamental enough in their own way none can compare with the original. It is possible that *E. wallichii* lurks in some enthusiast's garden and may even be found in the frames of a specialist grower waiting to be launched on the gardening public. I sincerely hope so.

As with all spurges, care should be exercised in handling *E. wallichii* lest its sap should accidentally stray onto one of the more sensitive parts of the body such as the mouth and eyes where its caustic nature will cause pain if not worse. It is best grown in a sheltered border preferably in a moist but well drained soil. In cold areas its emerging growth in spring may require the protection of straw or bracken to keep out frost. It associates well with blue flowers, especially moisture loving iris and in the Kashmir pastures it commonly grows with *Iris kamaonensis* and *I.* hookeriana, the patches and pools of blue creating an unforgettable contrast with the green and gold.

Glaucidium palmatum

From the moment I first set eyes on *Glaucidium palmatum*, I wanted to grow it in my own garden. It is one of the loveliest plants of its kind, possessing what some catalogues call a 'cool charm' typical of so many plants which in the wild inhabit mountain woodlands in the temperate zones of the northern hemisphere. Like so many choice woodlanders, this plant is a native of northern Japan where it is said to grow in high mountain forests. It is a perennial herb with a stout swollen rhizome and stout erect stem bearing two kidney-shaped or rounded, deeply, seven to eleven lobed and sharply toothed leaves up to 20cm (8in) across. Terminating the 45 to 60cm (18 to 24in) stem is a single, poppy-like flower 5 to 8cm (2 to 3in) across with four lavender-coloured petals and a central boss of yellow stamens. There is an equally beautiful form 'Leucanthum' with white flowers.

Glaucidium palmatum – *a choice Japanese woodlander. La Rochelle, New York (April).*

Both flower in late spring but even as a foliage plant, glaucidium is well worth growing, the descriptive name *palmatum* meaning 'lobed like a hand'. The leaves more resemble those of a large leaved maple.

Botanically, glaucidium is closely related both to the poppies and the podophyllums. It is sometimes placed in its own family (*Glaucidiaceae*) but is more commonly regarded as a member of the buttercup family (*Ranunculaceae*). Although hardy, it needs a cool, moist but well-drained leafy soil in light shade, sheltered from bright sun and cold winds. It is most at home in the woodland garden or peat bed where moisture is readily available during summer.

The stems continue to grow after flowering and in some situations can reach as much as 1 to 1.2m (3 to 4ft) tall. Even in seemingly ideal conditions *glaucidium* can suddenly 'fade away' for no apparent reason and one experienced plantswoman of my acquaintance firmly believes there to be an element of luck in its successful cultivation. This may be so but it is unlikely to deter keen gardeners from trying their hand at this most exquisite plant. It is increased either by careful division or by seeds though seedlings take several years to reach flowering maturity. Seed grown plants have flowers variable in depth of colour some being better than others.

Hacquetia epipactis

Glaucidium palmatum 'Leucanthum' *– a beautiful white flowered form. La Rochelle, New York (April).*

I never cease to be surprised by the strange bedfellows found in some of our well-known plant families. Take the umbels (*Umbelliferae*) for instance. It is easy to see a family likeness in the flowers of carrot, parsnip, Queen Ann's Lace and Ground Elder – the umbrella like heads are unmistakeable. When it comes to astrantia, however, the likeness is less obvious and in the sea hollies (*Eryngium* species) it is hard to believe. Examine the head of a Sea Holly, however, and it will be seen to be an umbel in which there are no stalks so that the individual flowers are crammed into a dense head. It is the same or almost so with *Hacquetia epipactis*, a small clump-forming herb from the east European alps, with toothed clover-shaped, bright green leaves.

From late winter into spring the stems emerge from just below the ground, eventually growing from 10 to 15cm (4 to 6in) tall. At the end of the stem is a bright, button-shaped head (umbel) of tiny yellow flowers surrounded by a collar of yellowish-green bracts turning to green with age. It is not unlike a winter aconite at a glance and follows that plant in flower. While by no means a show-stopper, this little plant is worth growing for its curiosity value and reliability in the early months of the year.

It is quite hardy and easy in most soils though it prefers a fertile, moist, but well-drained loam in light shade. It is an ideal plant for the peat garden or shady rock garden or even for the front of a border and once established is best left undisturbed although large clumps can, with care, be divided in autumn or winter. It can also be increased from seed. The name *Hacquetia* commemorates Balthasar Hacquet (1740–1815) an Austrian writer on Alpine plants.

Overleaf: Hacquetia epipactis – *a curious member of the carrot family. Burford House, Worcestershire (April).*

Lathraea clandestina

One of the most curious wild flowers I remember finding as a boy was the Toothwort – *Lathraea squammaria*, a parasite on the roots of hazel and certain other woody plants. Its creeping underground rhizomes are covered with fleshy, whitish, overlapping scales which resemble dentures, hence the common name and it taps into the sap layer of its host by means of special rootlets (haustoria). The only part of the plant to show above ground is the flower stem which bears a one sided spike of fleshy white, purple-tinged nodding flowers. It is more fascinating than attractive and not surprisingly is rarely seen in gardens. It has a relative, however, the so-called Blue Toothwort (*Lathraea clandestina*), which is very attractive and is sometimes seen in cultivation though not commonly. It is occasionally found growing away from gardens on the roots of willow and poplar by streams and generally in wet places but in such locations it is an introduction or garden escape being native only in Spain, Italy, west and central France and Belgium.

Unlike our native plant, *L. clandestina* does not produce a spike, but it carries its flowers in clusters at or just above ground level. They are produced singly from between the upper scales and being large and bright purple in colour are very conspicuous and ornamental. Indeed, when I was a student at the Cambridge University Botanic Garden in 1960–62 I was frequently asked by members of the public for the name of the 'blue crocus' growing near the lake there. The plant tends to form whitish scaly coral-like clumps which first make themselves known in February when they erupt from the soil surface. Then, in mid-spring earlier if the season is mild, the long-stalked, two-lipped flowers 5cm (2in) long emerge creating low mounds or patches of rich colour. Later, in late spring, the flowers die to be replaced by seed capsules which rupture on ripening, scattering their contents like buckshot over the surrounding area. The scaly clumps dry and blacken before quietly retreating below ground.

The name *clandestina* meaning 'hidden', refers to this plant's secretive lifestyle. I first saw it at Cambridge where it grew in the gardens on both willow and Silver Maple (*Acer saccharinum*). It had originally been planted and had escaped by means of its seeds being carried via a stream to the meadows outside, where it became established on native willow. Apart from an occasional frosting of the flowers in exposed sites, the Blue Toothwort is a hardy plant and one well worth trying in the garden if a suitable host is available. It is rarely ever catalogued and plants are best obtained from private or botanic garden sources by means of exchange.

I have established this plant several times on host plants by the following method. A clump of the toothwort is first lifted by means of a fork from an established colony. Care must be taken to include the rhizomes from beneath the soil. This operation is best carried out after flowering, especially when the seed capsules are ripening. Next, a strong root is exposed on a suitable host plant and the bark scratched or gently scraped to reveal the white tissue beneath. The toothwort clump is then placed on the injured root and covered over with soil. The operation completed it is probably best forgotten for it will take from two to three years for the toothwort to establish itself. It is probable that clumps will establish themselves if moved at flowering time but the later date ensures that ripe seed is also added to the site as a

Opposite: Lathraea clandestina – *a colourful perennial, here parasitic on willow. The Hillier Arboretum, Hampshire (April).*

safeguard. A small clump which I placed on the root of a hazel (*Cor*
avellana) in my garden four years ago suddenly – and to my g
surprise and delight – emerged and flowered last year.

If the host plant is growing strongly and is healthy it will no
unduly affected by the toothwort. Willows, Poplars and hazel
favourite hosts but other hosts would appear to be acceptable. T
Toothwort will grow preferably in shade in most ordinary gar
soils, acid or alkaline, being especially prolific in moist soils or th
which only become dry in summer.

Lobelia tupa

Caragh Lough is a wild stretch of water which lies within sigh
Carrauntoohil, Ireland's highest mountain in Macgillycuddy's Re
County Kerry. Its shallows are a home to an interesting selectio
native plants including the Water Lobelia – *Lobelia dortmanna*, wl
slender stems rise from their stony bed to carry the few delicate,
lilac flowers above the lough's surface. I first saw this uncommon p
here many years ago and more recently I again met with it at the e
of a stream within five minutes of that wonderful garden Inverew
Argyll. The non-botanist would find it hard to believe that W
Lobelia could have anything in common with the familiar l
bedding lobelia from South Africa and even less with the Sc
American *Lobelia tupa*, yet they all have the same flower parts albe
different size, colour and carriage. Visitors to Inverewe can see all tl
on the same day between Poolewe and the gardens and it is probabl
tupa, which grows so well at Inverewe and other west-coast gard
that will leave the most lasting impression.

It is a strong growing, erect perennial, in mild areas developir
woody base, with erect dark and dusky stems up to 2m (6ft). These
well clothed with lance-shaped, softly downy, light green leaves u
20cm (8in) long and terminate in a bold, spike-like raceme of redd
scarlet, curiously shaped flowers which open from the base upwa
The individual flowers, borne in reddish-purple cup-like calyces
tubular at first, the petals soon curving downwards to end in a cl
like limb, the segments joined at the tip. Meanwhile, the red stam
which are united into a tube, are thrust out above the petals ending
cluster of grey bearded anthers. They really are worth lookin
closely while an established clump in full flower has a bold
distinguished appearance recognizable from a distance.

It is a plant which enjoys a fertile soil with no lack of moistur
summer and a warm, sunny position is desirable. A plant in my gar
in Hampshire grows in a border at the foot of a south-facing dry st
wall where it flourishes. In an average spring, the young shoots
already apparent in early spring together with those of the herbac
peonies and in mid-summer are flowering to their hearts' content
colder inland areas it might benefit from some protection in wint
mulch of leaves, peat, bracken or straw sufficing although one gard
I know covers her plant with a cloche. It is seen at its best in wes
and southern areas of the British Isles and in mild pockets elsewh

In some situations, the stems may need some support to pre
them from leaning or falling over. This is best achieved by pla
short lengths of brushwood around the crown in spring allowing
stems to grow through.

Opposite: Lobelia tupa – *curious but*
colourful flowers. Author's garden,
Hampshire (July).

First introduced to British cultivation in 1824, *Lobelia tupa* is native to the Andes of Chile, *tupa* being the Chilean name for this plant. Its Spanish name is 'tabaco del diablo' ('devil's tobacco') the leaves being used as a narcotic and in medicine. It is increased by nurserymen from seed or from cuttings.

Lychnis × haageana

In my description of *Aralia elata* I have mentioned the Rock Garden in Moss Bank Park, Bolton where I first began work on leaving school. This garden provided my first introduction to a host of plants many of which, over 30 years later, are still among my favourites. One of these is a most spectacular campion *Lychnis × haageana*. We grew it then in a bed of ordinary soil to which we added plenty of grit to aid drainage. Other than that and a sunny site, it seemed none too fussy as to soil conditions as long as it was not waterlogged. It was a short lived perennial with weak, woolly hairy stems 30 to 45cm (12 to 18in) high and large flowers of a rich scarlet in summer. It was quite one of the most brilliantly coloured flowers I have ever seen.

It is a hybrid plant, its parents being the Japanese *L. sieboldii*, sometimes referred to as *L. coronata* var. *sieboldii* and *L. fulgens* which apart from Japan, is native also to Korea, north-east China and south-east Siberia. It flowers in summer from June onwards and it was in June 1984, on a trip to the Changbai Shan Forest Reserve in China's north-eastern Jilin Province, that I first saw *L. fulgens*, one of its parents. This was a taller plant to 60cm (2ft) or more with glowing scarlet flowers and long, deeply bifid petals. I shall never forget the sight of this impressive campion in its native home nor for that matter shall I forget the roadside scrub in which it grew and the numerous blood thirsty ticks which lurked there!

Lychnis × haageana is normally green stemmed, occasionally bronze or purple flushed. An even better plant to some minds is its hybrid with *L. chalcedonica*, the so-called Maltese Cross. This has been given the name *Lychnis × arkwrightii* no doubt—as in *L. haageana* – named after its raiser. The flowers are if anything, even bolder, of a vivid orange-red while a selection named 'Vesuvius' is said to be longer-lived with contrasting brownish leaves. All these campions are like caviar to slugs and snails and should be given the necessary protection to prevent them becoming chewed at the edges if not devoured.

They enjoy a moist but well-drained soil and it is prudent to have young plants in reserve, grown from seed or cuttings.

Melianthus major

Although often treated as a shrub in catalogues, *Melianthus major* is so often cut to the ground during severe winters that I feel it is best regarded as an herbaceous perennial in all but the mildest areas of the cool temperate zones. It is not reliably hardy in cold inland areas but in southern and western areas, where it is frequently damaged, it invariably sprouts anew from below ground each spring, its natural vigour soon making up for lost growth. It is cultivated mainly for its ornamental foliage borne on fleshy hollow, woody-based stems up to 2m (6ft) high. A well-established plant is an impressive sight with great

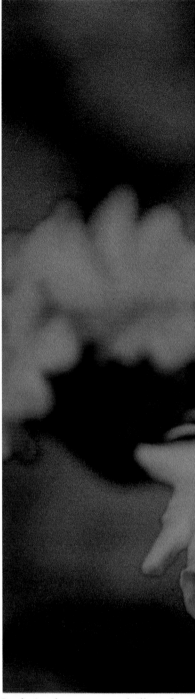

Lychnis × haageana – *a brilliant flame coloured campion. Author's garden, Hampshire (July).*

lush piles of deeply divided, ruffled and coarsely toothed leaves up to 45cm (18in) long which are smooth in texture and like the stems, a striking blue-green in colour. When bruised or broken, the leaves give off a foetid smell which in no way detracts from their visual merit.

In mild areas where stems survive the winter, long stalked racemes of brownish-red flowers with green stamens are produced in summer. More curious than beautiful, they add little if anything to the attraction of this plant. They are, however, well supplied with nectar which is a boon to the local insect population. In South Africa it is known as the Honey Flower.

Overleaf: Melianthus major — *a bold mound of striking foliage. Knightshayes Court, Devon (September).*

In some of the famous gardens of south-west Britain and Ireland *Melianthus major* is a regular summer attraction, especially when grown in a fertile, well-drained soil in full sun. Grown hard in a poor stony or sandy soil it is less luxuriant but longer lived. It looks particularly effective when planted in association with stone or red brick terraces, patios or in stone urns. It used to be a popular choice as a pot plant in subtropical bedding displays and is still occasionally seen used this way.

First introduced to Britain probably via Holland as long ago as 1688, it is native to South Africa where it is commonly found in dry stony places in the Cape Province. The descriptive name *major* meaning 'larger' is a comparison with *M. minor*, a similar but smaller relative. It is increased by nurserymen from seed or by cuttings.

Morina longifolia

Opposite: Morina longifolia – *flowers change colour as they mature. Author's garden, Hampshire (July).*

For many years I have grown *Morina longifolia* in my gardens, previously on the chalk of Winchester and now on an acid Bagshot sand. Its dense, evergreen, basal tufts of strap-shaped, spine toothed leaves suggest kinship with the thistles but nothing could be further from the truth. It is, in fact, a member of the teasel family (*Dipsacaceae*) though even this relationship is hard to swallow when you have both plants growing side by side. I first saw it in the mountains of East Nepal in 1971 where it grew on stony slopes on an exposed ridge. Much later, I found it again in the Himalaya, this time in Kashmir, where it grew in a ravine in the mountains above Gulmarg. There, it enjoyed a moist but well drained loamy soil in full sun and it appreciates similar conditions in the garden where, in summer, it produces stiffly erect stems bearing dense whorls of flowers in the axils of softly spiny bracts. The flowers occupy the upper half of the stem, forming an interrupted spike which lengthens as it matures, the flowers of the lower whorls opening first. The individual flowers are slender tubed and turn from white on first emerging, to rose and finally crimson, all three colours eventually represented on the one spike.

A well grown plant can produce spikes up to 1m (3ft) tall but generally they are 60cm (2ft) or less. The whole plant seems to bristle with soft spines occupying the leaf and bract margins. After flowering, the seed heads remain on the stems and turn brown, making them a useful addition to dried flower arrangements. A plant from wild collected Nepalese seed grows in a sunny border by my house where it has flowered for the last three years, each year seeing an increase in the number of spikes. It is a hardy perennial which responds well to good conditions and treatment including the occasional feeding. Nurserymen increase it from seed or by division. The name *longifolia* of course refers to the 'long leaves'.

Nicotiana sylvestris

I am unlikely ever to forget the tobacco plant, after all, it sparked off my interest in plants. The tobacco in question, however, was not the common kind but a Mexican tobacco *Nicotiana rustica*. I discovered it growing as a weed in a potato patch on an allotment near my school and climbed a fence to collect it. It was a leafy herb coated with clammy hairs while its flowers were lime green. I could not find it in

any flower book in the school library so I took it to my local museum whose staff were just as mystified as I was. Eventually, the plant (now pressed and dried) was sent to the British Museum (Natural History) in London from whence it was returned a week later with a letter attached giving its name and origin. The letter also informed me that not only was my discovery a new record for Lancashire but only the second record for this plant in Britain. I was 'over the moon' and from thenceforth my interest in bird watching changed to a passion for plant hunting.

I have seen and grown many other different nicotianas since then, most of them colourful and ornamental members of our garden flora such as the numerous garden varieties of *Nicotiana affinis*, especially 'Lime Green' and the Sensation strain. There are, however, two species which, although they have been around in cultivation for a long time, are now the subject of renewed interest mainly due to the activities of conservation minded gardeners and flower arrangers. One of these is *N. sylvestris*, a native of Argentina, first introduced to the west in 1898. Although in warm sheltered spots or in mild winters it is a short lived perennial, it is normally treated as an annual or biennial, seed being sown under glass in late winter and the seedlings hardened off before planting out in their final position in late spring or early summer. This is certainly the best way of growing it in cold areas. Alternatively, it may be grown in pots for the summer patio or conservatory.

Above: Nicotiana langsdorffii – *lime green flowers in loose heads. Author's garden, Hampshire (August).*

Opposite: Nicotiana sylvestris – *bold pyramids of fragrant flowers. Burford House Gardens, Worcestershire (August).*

N. sylvestris is a stout plant with an erect stem to 1.4m (5ft) clothed in the lower half with large green leaves, larger towards the base. Above the leaves rises a bold-flowering stem (panicle) of white, long-tubed nodding flowers 9cm (3½in) long which are deliciously fragrant especially in the evening, attracting a regular moth clientele. Until the recent spate of severe winters, this magnificent tobacco persisted in my garden and even now, I find odd seedlings appearing each summer in sheltered corners. In my opinion it is quite the most impressive of the species in general cultivation although by no means common. There is nothing to match its marvellous scented pyramids of white bloom soaring above mounds of bold foliage. The entire plant is covered with clammy hairs.

Different again is *N. langsdorffii*, a native of Brazil first introduced as long ago as 1819. Although it can reach similar heights to *N. sylvestris* it is a much more branching slender-stemmed plant with smaller leaves The flowers are produced in loose clusters towards the ends of the branches unlike the dense clusters of the other. Individually, they are 2.5 to 3cm (1 to 1¼in) long, nodding and tubular, the tube swollen below the shallowly cup-shaped mouth. In colour they are lime-green with the turqoise-blue anthers crowding the mouth. The whole plant is clammy hairy while the flowers are scentless. Cultivation is the same as for *N. sylvestris*. Both species appreciate a fertile, well-drained soil in a warm, sunny site where they will flower from late summer into autumn or in the case of *N. langsdorffii*, until the first frosts.

Both may be used singly as accent plants among low annuals or perennials or in groups in mixed perennial borders. *N. sylvestris* is particularly impressive when planted in bold drifts where its flowers and its scent can be enjoyed from the house, while children love to watch visiting moths from an open window. In the case of *N. sylvestris*, a too rich soil can produce plants with more leaf than flower which is to be avoided.

The name *sylvestris* meaning 'of woods' suggests a woodland habitat in the wild and this plant will certainly tolerate light or dappled shade. The name *langsdorffii* commemorates Georg Heinrich von Langsdorff (1774–1852) a German botanist who collected in Brazil.

Pancratium illyricum

Most years I receive letters from gardeners recently returned from Mediterranean resorts telling me about this or that strange or beautiful plant seen on their holiday in the sun. They often enclose photographs and occasionally the photograph depicts *Pancratium maritimum*, the so-called Sea Daffodil or Sea Lily flowering on a sandy sea shore (*maritimum* –'pertaining to the sea'). In the same family as the daffodil (*Amaryllidaceae*), *P. maritimum* bears its white, richly fragrant, long tubed flowers in an umbel from the top of a stout stem up to 40cm (16in) tall. They are accompanied by the long pointed strap-shaped greyish or sea green leaves which persist through winter.

Flowering takes place from July to September and a colony in full flower in its native sand-dunes is a sight not easily forgotten. It grows from a large bulb which is said to be slightly poisonous while the ancient Greeks claimed it possessed tonic properties. It is occasionally seen in gardens in mild areas where it requires a warm, sunny, well-drained situation to thrive. A hardier species and one more suitable for

Opposite: Pancratium illyricum – *sun loving perennial for well drained site. Cambridge University Botanic Garden (June).*

general cultivation is *Pancratium illyricum*, although this too requires similar conditions of cultivation. It is more local in its distribution than *P. maritimum*, restricted to the islands of Corsica, Sardinia and Capri where it is found among shady rocks at low altitudes, generally near the sea. It is also more robust than the other with broader, herbaceous leaves and flowering stems up to 45cm (18in) or more. The fragrant white flowers borne in umbels in late spring and early summer are 6 to 9cm (2 to 4in) long, short-tubed and have spreading lance-shaped segments.

First introduced to Britain in 1615, *P. illyricum* remains uncommon in cultivation here other than in specialist collections and botanic gardens. The finest plant I have seen grew on the Limestone Rock Garden in the Cambridge University Botanic Garden where it occupied a sunny pocket between two large boulders. Although by no means hardy, it is certainly well worth trying in a warm sunny position such as the foot of a south or south-west facing wall. Young bulbs can be expected to flower within two to three years given suitable conditions. Alternatively, they may be increased from seed, a slower process.

The name *illyricum*, 'of Illyria', refers to a region roughly corresponding to western Jugoslavia and comprising Liburnia and Dalmatia.

Rodgersia pinnata

The name *Rodgersia* commemorates an American, Rear-Admiral John Rodgers who between 1852 and 1856 commanded a Pacific expedition during which the first member of this group of perennials was discovered. This was the Japanese species *Rodgersia podophylla* which Rodgers' party collected at Hokodote on the 13th June 1877. Since then, five other species have been recognized mainly from the Chinese mainland, whilst a sixth species *R. tabularis*, is now regarded as belonging to a separate genus *Astilboides*. All are bold foliaged, hardy perennials differing from one another mainly in leaf characteristics.

Rodgersia pinnata is one of the most satisfactory and easily recognized species in cultivation, its leaves divided into several leaflets, leathery in texture and boldly net-veined. Despite the name, the leaves are not truly pinnate (as in those of an ash), the majority of leaflets being borne on a short axis from the top of the main stalk which is stout and up to 1m (3ft) tall. The pyramidal plumes of tiny crowded flowers rise above the leaf canopy during summer to give an impressive display.

In colour they are pink in bud paling to cream with or without a pink tint when fully open. There is also a white flowered form 'Alba' and a choice form named 'Superba' with flowers of a rich pink whose stalks and young leaves are an attractive bronze-red. The flowers give way to seed capsules which in some forms darken to reddish as they mature.

There are few more handsome flowering and foliage plants for the waterside than the Rodgersias and *R. pinnata* is one of the most satisfactory, especially when planted in bold drifts. It enjoys a moist soil in sun or light shade but any ordinary garden soil will suffice as long as sufficient moisture is available in the summer. It does not thrive in dry, exposed situations nor should it be planted in the depth of a shrubbery where its beauty will be marred if not ruined by too close competition. In the wild, *R. pinnata* grows by streams, in damp depressions and in

Rodgersia pinnata – *frothy pink plumes over bold foliage. Mount Stewart, N. Ireland (July).*

moist woodland situations in the mountains of south-west China (Yunnan). In places, it forms extensive colonies and must be a magnificent spectacle when flowering is at its peak.

It is increased by nurserymen from seed or by division.

Roscoea auriculata

The roscoeas are hardy members of the ginger family (*Zingiberaceae*), their name commemorating William Roscoe (1753–1831) one of the founders of the Liverpool Botanic Garden who had a special interest in this family. There are 17 species presently recognized, native to the Himalaya from Kashmir eastwards to Assam and in south-west China.

Overleaf: Roscoea '*Beesiana*' — *a magnificent colony of this lovely perennial. Bressingham Gardens, Norfolk (July).*

I saw one of these, *R. purpurea*, in September 1971 flowering among scrub on a mountain above Kathmandu in Nepal. Its purple flowers were visible from some distance but it was only when the track I was following wound its way through the roscoeas that I was able to appreciate their beauty more closely. It was under the name *R. purpurea* that another roscoea was introduced to western cultivation by J. D. Hooker from his expedition to Sikkim in the middle of the last century. This too, had purple flowers but it was subsequently found to differ in a number of ways from *R. purpurea* and was eventually given the name *R. auriculata*, a reference to the ear-like lobes (auricles) at the base of the leaf blade.

R. auriculata is not uncommon in cultivation though it is still commonly catalogued and grown as *R. purpurea* or as var. *procera*. It is a hardy and relatively easy perennial requiring a cool, moist but well-drained, preferably humus-rich, soil in sun or light shade. From a tuberous rootstock arise erect fleshy stems 40cm (16in) or more tall, clothed with bold green, lance-shaped leaves and ending in a spike of fleshy green bracts. From out of these bracts emerge a succession of long-tubed, large orchid-like flowers throughout summer coloured a rich violet-purple. Rarely are more than two flowers open on one spike at the same time but the effect is nonetheless striking. It is without question, one of the most exotic looking of all hardy perennials and is worth preparing a pocket of soil specially to suit it.

Other roscoeas are equally beautiful including the yellow flowered *R. cautleoides* from south-west China while in *Roscoea* 'Beesiana' we have an unusual plant – possibly a hybrid between *R. auriculata* and *R. cautleioides* in which the lip of the yellow flower is sometimes suffused, or streaked, buff and lilac. A drift of this plant in full flower is an arresting sight in late summer.

All the roscoeas are increased by nurserymen either from seed or by division. The rootstocks should be planted up to 12.5cm (5in) deep and should then be left alone. They are naturally late into growth and on no account should the soil above their crowns be disturbed until the shoots make their appearance in early summer. From then on growth is rapid. In the acid sand of my Hampshire garden several roscoeas grow, their positions in winter marked by a short stick or cane. Their late emergence ensures that they avoid damage from late frosts and they provide the garden with some of its most colourful splashes during the summer season.

Sanguinaria canadensis 'Flore Pleno'

My very first visit to North America took place during the winter of 1975/76 on the invitation of the American Rock Garden Society. I was to give a talk at a meeting they had arranged in Boston and no amount of snow was going to prevent me from accomplishing that pleasant task. During my stay in Massachusetts, I was taken to see the Garden in the Woods run by the New England Wild Flower Society at Framlingham where the curator showed me round. All that I could see were ghostly birch and the dead tops of herbs protruding from the deep snow but my host more than made up for this in describing the rich tapestry of native flowers that would follow the spring thaw. On my leaving, she made me a gift of a little book describing the wild flowers of the Eastern American deciduous forest. In this book each flower is illustrated by a colour photograph and I have rarely seen anything so evocative of an earthly paradise. One of the photographs depicts the Bloodroot *Sanguinaria canadensis* whose names refer to the bright reddish or orange sap which exudes from the rhizome when it is cut or broken. It was one of the plants lying snug beneath the snow at Framlingham that was brought so vividly to life by the curator.

Despite two subsequent visits to the eastern states and Canada I have yet to see the bloodroot's flowers peppering the woodland floors though I have seen them often enough in gardens where this plant is not uncommon having first been introduced into cultivation as long ago as 1680. It is a member of the poppy family (*Papaveraceae*) to which also belongs, incidentally, the Chinese Plume Poppy (*Macleaya*) whose sap is similarly coloured. From the long thick underground rhizome in early spring rise the young growths which erupt through the soil surface like grey-purple mushrooms. Development is fairly rapid and soon the 'mushroom' reveals itself as a leaf in which the flower bud is wrapped. In seemingly no time at all, the flower has opened displaying a ring of eight to ten fragile white petals around a cluster of yellow stamens and styles. Meanwhile the handsome blue-grey, kidney-shaped leaf begins to expand showing off its lobed and prettily scalloped margin. The flowers are beautiful but fleeting and soon the petals lie on the ground while the leaves continue to grow.

It is a choice, hardy, dwarf plant for a moist but well-drained soil and seems equally happy in sun or light shade. Even better, however, is the fully double form 'Flore Pleno' whose flowers, like small peonies rise above the leaves on fleshy, 10cm (4in), violet-flushed stems. Being double, the flower is naturally longer lasting making this plant one of the most desirable of all spring flowering perennials. A nice clump of 'Flore Pleno' is flourishing in the acid sandy soil of my garden, increasing with each passing year. It originated from a garden in upper New York State where it formed gorgeous carpets in woodland.

The bloodroot can be increased by seed or division while the last named method is the only way of increasing 'Flore Pleno'. Given the right conditions, they will form a clump or patch and are then quite stunning in flower against the dark, bare earth. Care should be taken when working around the Bloodroot in winter or spring before its new growths appear. The rhizomes and the awakening shoots are easily damaged by a probing spade, trowel or fork.

As the descriptive name suggests, *Sanguinaria canadensis* is native to Canada as well as to the USA being a common woodlander in the eastern provinces and states.

Saxifraga umbrosa

One day several years ago, I was visiting Brian Halliwell, Curator of the Alpine and Herbaceous Department at Kew Gardens, delivering a box of plants which I had grown from seed collected in the wild. He took me through a back door into the Alpine nursery, a mouth watering experience for any plantsman and left the plants in the care of his assistant Tony Hall. He then asked if there was anything I would like in exchange, a dangerous invitation and I looked hopefully in the direction of a saxifrage in a pot. It stood, seemingly neglected in a corner and belonged to the evergreen London Pride group. Brian willingly gave me a small plant of the saxifrage which he told me was

Sanguinaria canadensis 'Flore Pleno' – *one of the most beautiful of all double flowered perennials. Author's garden, Hampshire (April).*

the true *S. umbrosa*, a native of the western and central Pyrenees.

The name is more commonly attached to the 'London Pride' —*Saxifraga × urbium*, a well known garden hybrid between true *S. umbrosa* and *S. spathularis*, a mountain plant of northern Portugal and north-west Spain. *S. spathularis* is also found in the west of Ireland where it is known as 'St. Patrick's Cabbage'. I first saw this plant in the wild mountain country around Killarney in County Kerry where it grows on damp rocks and on the banks of roadside ditches. *Saxi-*

fraga × urbium (the name meaning 'of towns') on the other hand is a long time resident of our gardens though exactly when, where and in what circumstances it arose is not recorded. It well earns its English name as a tenacious and reliable garden plant tolerant of most soils and situations, even neglect. It is one of the first plants I can remember from my childhood as it lined the path to the front door of my home and grew on the mound of boulders my grandfather called his rock garden.

The tight rosettes of leathery, toothed, spoon-shaped leaves formed dense hummocks and carpets which seemed to last forever while the small starry white flowers with a reddish central stain were borne in branched heads (panicles) on glandular downy stems up to 30cm (12in) high. These appeared without fail from late spring into early summer and gave rise to a curious warning from my mother that we should not discard our warm clothing until the flowers of London Pride were over. A better known version is 'never cast a clout (an article of clothing) 'till May is out'.

There are numerous forms of *S. × urbium* including *primuloides*, in effect, a miniature version with bright pink flowers. This is said to be a wild variety from the Pyrenees which brings me back to *S. umbrosa*. The Kew plant thrived in my garden and when I moved to my present garden I brought it with me, together with 300 or so other plants. It is less robust than *S. × urbium* with smaller leaves lined with horny teeth. The flowering stems, while just as sticky and reddish, are shorter while the starry white flowers are marked with numerous red dots giving the flowers a decided reddish appearance. It is a cheerful and reliable plant of its kind although it is at present only available from a few specialist nurserymen who increase it by division.

All members of this group make excellent ground cover in shade forming, dense, evergreen carpets – the name *umbrosa* means 'shade-loving'. Such is the variation of leaf shape, size and hairiness that they make pleasing and often striking contrasts when planted together. They may also be effectively grown with other carpeting perennials such as *Ajuga reptans*, *Lysimachia nummularia* 'Aurea' and stonecrops (Sedum species) such as *S. ewersii*, *S. kamschaticum*, *S. spurium* and *S. pulchellum*.

Sisyrinchium douglasii

To most plant enthusiasts, the name David Douglas is synonymous with trees, especially conifers exemplified by *Pseudotsuga menziesii*, the Douglas Fir. Born to a Scottish stonemason at Scone in Perthshire in 1799, Douglas showed an early interest in natural history and it is not surprising that he chose to follow a career in horticulture. In 1823, under the aegis of the Royal Horticultural Society, he made his first visit to North America with the intention of collecting and studying plants both wild and cultivated in New England. This however, was a tame preliminary to further assignments which were to take him on a series of journeys in western North America from British Columbia to California. His adventures during the next ten years are the stuff that boys dream about. Shooting rapids in a canoe, climbing mountains and dodging unfriendly Indians were all part of a day's work and in the intervals between the more hair-raising incidents, he collected plants many of which had not previously been seen by the scientific world.

The seeds of pines and firs, spruces and maples and a host of shrubs he

Opposite: Saxifraga umbrosa – a parent of the well known London Pride. Author's Garden, Hampshire (June).

Opposite: Sisyrinchium douglasii —
*rich purple bells in early spring. The
Hillier Arboretum, Hampshire
(March).*

despatched home to the gardens and estates of Britain, but it was not only woody plants that caught Douglas's attention. Although less often remembered today, he was responsible for introducing a far greater number of non-woody plants, annuals and perennials, one of which was *Sisyrinchium douglasii* sometimes, though incorrectly, referred to by the equally appropriate name *S. grandiflorum*. Douglas introduced this charming little plant in 1826 having found it on the low hills of the Columbia River area between, to quote Douglas, 'the Great Falls and Onkanagan'.

Known as Spring Bell in the wild, this hardy perennial has a creeping rootstock from which erect flattened shoots 20 to 25cm (8 to 10in) tall bearing two to three narrow pointed leaves with a sheathing base arise early in the year. The flowers appear in early spring, bursting from between two protective bracts (a spathe) at the stem's summit. They are bell-shaped, 1.5 to 2cm ($\frac{1}{2}$ to $\frac{3}{4}$in) long with six segments of a beautiful reddish-purple colour, the stamens with bright orange anthers. From two to six flowers are produced from each spathe, hanging free on threadlike stalks and trembling in the slightest breeze. As in most other sisyrinchiums, the flowers are fully open only in sunshine. After flowering, the whole plant dies down to below ground level and its position needs to be carefully marked to avoid risk of accident.

In the wild it ranges from British Columbia south to Nevada and California where it occurs on prairies and rocky slopes from sea level up to 1800m (6,000ft). In cultivation it enjoys a moist but well-drained soil, the presence of moisture being particularly important in spring when the plant is in growth. I have seen it grown successfully on the rock garden or scree as well as in the peat garden in sun or dappled shade.

In a group (genus) of plants containing the good, the bad and the ugly, *Sisyrinchium douglasii* lays claim to being the most beautiful and is one of those plants which Reginald Farrer chose to eulogize in his classic work *The English Rock Garden*, lavishing on it some of his finest superlatives. These are his final words 'It is so breathtaking a beauty in its Byzantine magnificence of colour and fineness of its Coan texture, that one can hardly turn away to look at the white variety, which is lovely and delicate and lustrous in its way as a sunlit pearl in dreamland.' The white form 'Alba' is occasionally available and is well worth growing together with the typical plant and after the above description, who can resist? They are increased by nurserymen from seed or division and are grown for sale in pots.

Stipa gigantea

Like so many excellent plants, I first came across *Stipa gigantea* in the Hillier Arboretum in the 1960s. We had received its seeds from a botanical garden source and from the resultant seedlings three youngsters were planted out in a simulated dry steam bed, a long depression excavated by hand in the acid sand and mulched with gravel. They flourished in the sun and good drainage, in time combining to form a bold clump of long, narrow, green leaves. The crowning glory of this ornamental grass however comes in summer with the numerous erect stems (culms) up to 2.5m (8ft) bearing at their summit showers (panicles) of large purplish spikelets to 2.5cm (1in) long, their length and beauty increased by two long bristles (awns) up to 7.5cm (3in) or

Above: Stipa gigantea – *a bold ornamental grass from sunny Spain. The Hillier Arboretum, Hampshire (July).*

Thalictrum delavayi – *the contrasting white stamens and purple petals. Author's garden, Hampshire (August).*

more. The spikelets are the chief ornament of *Stipa gigantea* and present a long season of interest from the early summer purple to a shining golden yellow. Even when the seeds have been shed there is beauty in the empty husks which remain on the stems, a pale straw yellow.

On an established plant, the flower heads of this grass are magnificent, great loosely conical heads of nodding, long-awned spikelets which shimmer in the sun and tremble at the slightest breeze. In the wild it is found in grassy or stony places in Spain, Portugal and Morocco and in cultivation it seems to require nothing more than good drainage and plenty of sun. It is best planted as a specimen or in groups of three or five in a bed in the lawn or with other, smaller grasses. I have seen it used to great effect on patios and in courtyards relishing the reflected sun and warmth. It is increased by nurserymen from seed or by division.

Thalictrum delavayi

Most keen gardeners can name, without recourse to books, at least one Chinese tree or shrub which was originally introduced to the west by E. H. Wilson. When it comes to perennials, however, the result is likely to be different. Wilson was a plant hunter of wide interests, as his collections of *Acer griseum*, *Kolkwitzia amabilis*, *Picea wilsonii*, *Lilium regale* and *Primula pulverulenta* testify, yet it is a sad fact that the great majority of his perennial introductions have been lost to cultivation. One of the happy exceptions is *Thalictrum delavayi* which is named after the French missionary Jean Delavay who was the first to find this plant in Yunnan.

Wilson's introduction was at first given the name *T. dipterocarpum* (with two-winged fruits) but was subsequently considered to be the same as that found by Delavay. It is a magnificent plant of its kind, forming bold piles of dainty, much-divided leaves from out of which rise tall stems up to 1.5m (5ft) or more bearing large airy branching heads (panicles) of rich lilac flowers with protruding cream coloured anthers in summer. Its one weakness is that its top-heavy stems are apt to break when exposed to strong gusts so *T. delavayi* must be given shelter or alternatively some form of support such as pieces of brushwood placed around the root crown in spring before growth is advanced. Another method is to grow this plant among small shrubs through which its stems can rise.

In September 1986 I saw this plant west of Kumning, in central Yunnan where it grew in some numbers on scrub covered sunny hillsides above the road. There, its stems reached 2m (6ft) supporting huge pyramidal heads of flower and providing the only colour in an otherwise arid looking landscape. I was further interested to see the dry, poor soil conditions enjoyed by the above plants. When in cultivation, *T. delavayi* responds best to a rich, deep soil in sun or light shade. There is a beautiful white flowered form 'Album' occasionally offered by specialist nurseries and a double form known as 'Hewitt's Double' named after the now defunct Hewitt Nursery of Solihull, Birmingham, which is where the young Wilson began his working life. Perhaps this form arose from Wilson's original seed or much later as a seedling sport. Its flowers have many petals crowded into a tiny rosette. Longer lasting than those of the typical plant, they lack the contrasting cream-coloured anthers. 'Hewitt's Double' is also less hardy than the type and unless protected can be lost during severe winters, especially where soil conditions are heavy and wet.

T. delavayi is increased by nurserymen from seed or by division, 'Album' and 'Hewitt's Double' by division or cuttings.

Veratrum album

Above: Veratrum album – *bold perennial of stately appearance. Raby Castle, Northumbria (August).*

Anything more unlike a lily would be hard to imagine but ignoring the general appearance of the plant and looking closely at the flowers the similarities are there to be seen, to a botanist's eye certainly. Known as the False or White Hellebore, *Veratrum album* has been in cultivation since 1650 at least, though it is by no means as common as its merit deserves. It is native to northern temperate regions of Europe and Asia where it is found in mountain meadows and clearings in woodland. It is a robust perennial forming bold clumps of stout erect leafy stems to 2m (6ft), the leaves bold and handsomely veined, largest at the base decreasing in size upwards. Each stem ends in a large branched head (panicle) of greenish-white, six-petalled flowers which are densely crowded on the panicle branches during late summer.

It is an impressive plant when established, outstanding in the mixed perennial border but even better when treated as an isolated group in a bed. The descriptive name *album* refers to the whitish flowers while in *V. nigrum* and *V. viride* the flowers are respectively maroon and green. All three are available from specialist nurserymen and each in its own way is indispensible in all but the smallest garden, being quite hardy, dying down to below ground in autumn and suitable for a moist but well drained soil. The best foliage effects are obtained on plants grown in a cool, deep, rich soil in light shade.

They are increased by nurserymen from seed or by careful division, seedlings taking several years to reach flowering maturity. The rhizomes of *V. album* are extremely poisonous and were once used dried and crushed as 'Hellebore Powder' to destroy caterpillars.

Viola 'Jackanapes'

Garden plant varieties named after people are commonplace, *Dianthus* 'Mrs Sinkins', *Aubrieta* 'Dr. Mules' and *Geum* 'Dolly North' being three of the best known. Plants named after animals, however, are not common and one named after a pet monkey probably unique. Strange though it may seem, such is the origin of the name *Viola* 'Jackanapes'. The plant itself seems to have appeared round about 1885 and was named by Gertrude Jekyll after a monkey which apparently sat on her shoulders during forays into her garden at Munstead Wood in Surrey. Whether Gertrude Jekyll actually raised the viola or acquired it from another source I have been unable to discover. Whatever the answer, this is one of the most colourful and cheerful looking violas I know.

It is a perennial herb of bushy habit up to 23cm (9in), free flowering and continuous from late spring into summer. The three lower petals of the flower are yellow while the two upper petals are chocolate brown, a striking combination. According to Richard Cawthorne, a life-long admirer and grower of violas, it was probably the result of a hybrid between an unknown garden viola and *Viola tricolor*, the native Heartsease.

Viola *'Jackanapes' – bicolor named after a pet monkey. Waterperry Horticultural College, Oxfordshire (May).*

In 1981 Cawthorne raised a seedling from 'Jackanapes' which he named 'Iver Grove' after the small mansion in Iver, Buckinghamshire where Lord Gambier's gardener Thompson made the original crossings of *V. tricolor* in 1813, from which all the garden pansies and violas originated. *Viola* 'Iver Grove' is similar in habit and colouring to 'Jackanapes' but has two chocolate brown spots on the lower yellow petals.

Both are increased from cuttings and prefer cool conditions in the garden with light shade and a moist, but well-drained, fertile soil. Unless it is intended to sow the seed to produce seedlings of unknown qualities the faded flowers are best cut away before the capsules develop while a general light pruning in autumn will help keep the plant compact. They respond well to feeding with a general, preferably organic, fertilizer and should be guarded against both slugs and greenfly which can be particularly troublesome.

Watsonia beatricis

In the warmer areas of Britain and North America where long cold winters are not a regular event, the watsonias of South Africa offer a wide range of colourful flowers lasting through the summer months sometimes into autumn. They are members of the Iris family (*Iridaceae*) related to the gladiolus with similar corms at the base. *Watsonia beatricis* in my experience is one of the hardiest of those in general cultivation though it still enjoys – and should be given – a warm situation in a moist but well-drained soil. I have seen it so grown in several gardens where it is often situated at the base of a south or south-west facing wall for extra winter protection. In one such place it flourishes in my garden forming dense clumps of evergreen arching, iris-like leaves from which rise the flowering stems up to 1m (3ft) tall. These carry a two-rowed spike of funnel-shaped flowers spreading widely at the mouth into six segments.

Variable in colour from pink to apricot and red, the one most commonly seen, in Britain certainly, has flowers coral red with a white flare on the two lateral segments. Flowering begins in summer and on a large, well-established plant continues into early autumn. In mild climates the range of watsonias available is large and apart from the many species there are numerous hybrids, several of which are occasionally offered by specialist nurserymen. Some gardens have their own special strains among which the Tresco Hybrids are occasionally seen in Britain's west coast gardens. These originated in the Tresco Abbey Garden in the Isles of Scilly towards the end of the last century.

In the wild, *W. beatricis* is found in an area receiving plenty of rain throughout the year. In cultivation, therefore, it does not do to plant it in a dry soil. Sun it will take, light shade even, but it needs sufficient moisture in spring, prior to growth and during the summer when in flower. Plants grown in a well-drained sunny situation, such as that at the base of a wall, should not be allowed to dry out during the spring and summer period. Such situations are best specially prepared before planting, digging out any rubble that may be present and filling the hole with a moisture-retentive compost mixed with coarse grit.

All watsonias may be grown either from seed or by division, the last named method ensuring stock which is true to type. The name *beatricis* commemorates Beatrix Hops who first discovered this plant.

Watsonia beatricis – *South African relative of the gladiolus. The Hillier Arboretum, Hampshire (July).*

Zauschneria cana

In October 1985 I was fortunate enough to be shown the so-called Californian Fuchsia *Zauschneria californica* in the wild for the first time. It was towards the end of a mind-boggling four day, 1,000 mile round journey of exploration in California organized for me by Wayne Roderick of San Francisco, an authority on the Californian flora. I had been travelling with Wayne in his faithful old transit, camping at night beneath ponderosa and pinyon pines and by day soaking up new and wonderful experiences. At one point, low on the western slopes of the High Sierras, we stopped by the roadside to admire a magnificent panorama of rock and trees. Growing on the loose sandy slope beneath our feet was the zauschneria, still with a few flowers.

I had first seen this plant in a rock garden in Lancashire when I was a young man and seeing it in its native habitat brought back pleasant memories. Sometimes listed in nurserymen's catalogues under shrubs, the zauschnerias are really subshrubs in that their stems develop a woody base. Normally, however, they are cut back in cold winters and behave as an herbaceous perennial. Naturally, considering their homeland, they love the sun and hot dry conditions but may be grown quite successfully in the cool temperate areas as long as their rootstock is well protected. To achieve this, the plant may be protected with a gravel mulch or planted among large stones or rocks beneath which its roots may freely develop.

Zauschneria cana – loose sprays of slender scarlet flowers. Knightshayes Court, Devon (September).

Even better are those individuals planted in a dry wall into which they can retreat during severe winters and from out of which they emerge to welcome the sun in summer. I have a plant of *Z. californica* 'Glasnevin' in a dry wall in my garden which behaves perfectly satisfactorily this way and flowers profusely over many weeks of summer and autumn. I also grow *Z. cana* (cana = grey) a densely branched bushy plant up to 45cm (18in), the stems clothed with small thread-like, silvery-grey leaves. Above these in summer rise sprays of slender scarlet flowers in striking contrast to the grey foliage. *Z. californica* is similar but with leaves variable in width and colour from green to grey-green. In 'Glasnevin' the leaves are dark green and the flowers a richer scarlet.

In colder areas they are sometimes treated as a summer bedding subject, grown with other similar plants in beds, borders or urns before being lifted for winter. Their flower colour is outstanding when associated with any silver or grey foliaged perennial, especially the smaller artemisias and ballotas and the trailing helichrysums. They are increased by nurserymen from cuttings or seed.

A—Z of Plants

The purpose of the following list is to provide a rapid reference to the plants described in this book. Details of height, flowering period etc. should be taken as approximate under average conditions. The column giving North American hardiness zones is likewise merely a guide and in no way replaces the solid and more reliable advice to be had from local experience and expertise. The information on hardiness zones by the way is mainly derived from Dirr, Rehder, Wharton, Wyman and Hortus Third.

The numbers represent the coldest zones in which these plants can reasonably be expected to succeed (see map for location of zones).

Key: **T** = Tree
     P = Perennial
     CL = Climber
     S = Shrub
     B = Biennial
     Co = Conifer

Opposite: Map showing the hardiness zones of North America Temperate ranges

HARDINESS ZONE
TEMPERATURE RANGES

°F	ZONE	°C
below −50	1	below −45
−50 to −40	2	−45 to −40
−40 to −30	3	−40 to −34
−30 to −20	4	−34 to −29
−20 to −10	5	−29 to −23
−10 to 0	6	−23 to −17
0 to 10	7	−17 to −12
10 to 20	8	−12 to −7
20 to 30	9	−7 to −1
30 to 40	10	−1 to 5

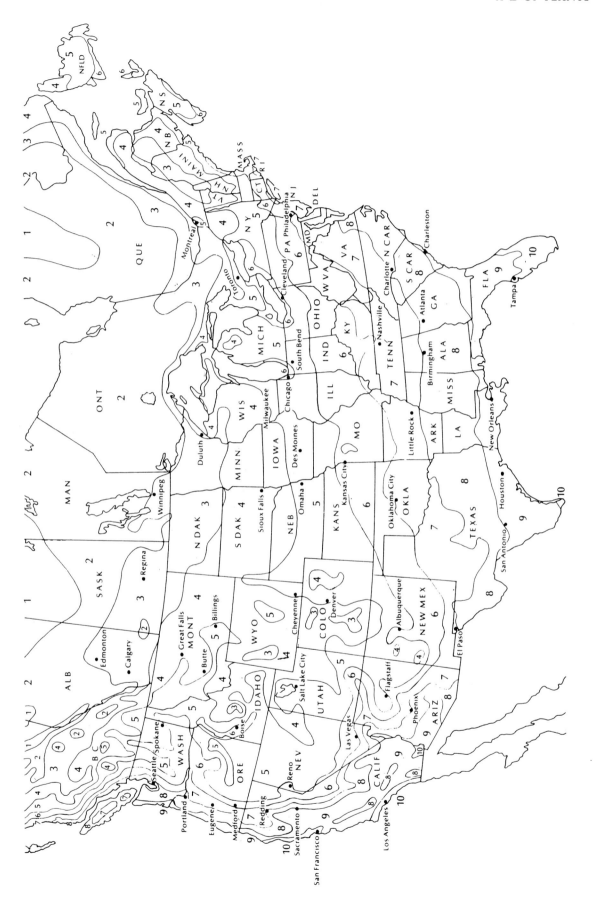

Plant name (description)	Average height	Soil and situation (ideally)	Hardiness UK	Hardiness Zone, North America	Flowers	Leaves (deciduous unless otherwise indicated)	Fruits, bark etc.
Acer griseum (T)	10 m (32 ft) +	moist, but well drained; open	hardy	4		three leaflets, colours well in autumn	Bark: outstanding feature – paper-thin and peels
Acer 'Silver Vein' (T)	4.5 to 6 m (15 to 20 ft)	moist, but well drained; open	hardy	5		fine foliage, large, colours well in autumn	Bark: white, pale green or grey vertical striations
Acer triflorum (T)	10 m (32 ft) +	moist, but well drained; open	hardy	5		3 leaflets, colourful in autumn	Bark: ornamental, dark, peeling
Actaea rubra (P)	45 cm (18 in)	moisture-retentive half shade	hardy	3	spring – white in dense heads	deeply divided	Berries: bright red, dense clusters, summer/autumn
Actinidia kolomikta (Cl)	7 m (22 ft) +	moist, but well drained; open	hardy	4	creamy white, late spring	summer – heart-shaped, large 7.5 to 15 cm (3 to 6 in) strikingly variegated	
Aesculus californica (T)	4.5 m (15 ft)	well drained; open	hardy	7	summer – white, erect, cylindrical spikes	5–7 fingered, glossy, metallic green	Bark: flaking; Fruit: huge conkers 7.5 cm (3 in) across
Allium cernuum (P) (bulb)	45 cm (18 in)	well drained; open	hardy	2	summer – drooping, terminal heads, bell-shaped, various shades of purple	grass-like	
Alnus firma (T)	12 m (40 ft)	moist; open	hardy	5	spring – drooping yellow catkins	impressive, 11.5 cm (4½ in), numerous veins	Bark: dappled, flaking

	Height	Soil/situation	Hardiness	Zone	Flowering	Foliage/leaves	Fruit/bark
Anemonella thalictroides 'Schoaff's Double' (P)	15 to 18 cm (6 to 8 in)	moist, but well drained, partial shade	hardy	4	spring – pale pink, double	deeply divided	
Aralia elata 'Variegata' (T)	3.5 m (12 ft) +	most; open	hardy	3	late summer to early autumn – creamy-white	large, variegated, divided into numerous leaflets	Fruit: autumn, tiny, purple-black
Arbutus × andrachnoides (T)	10 m (32 ft)	well drained; open	sun and warmth essential	7	late autumn to early spring – white, pitcher-shaped	evergreen	Fruit: red, small Bark: rich dark red, peeling
Arisaema sikokianum (P)	45 cm (18 in)	cool, moist but well drained, partial shade	hardy in a sheltered site	6	spring to early summer – solitary, dark purple with white interior	long-stalked with 3 leaflets	
Ballota pseudodictamnus (P)	60 cm (2 ft)	well drained, in full sun	not for cold areas	8–9	summer – white	grey, woolly	
Betula albo-sinensis (T)	20 m (65 ft)	moist but open	hardy	3		slender, pointed	Bark: thin, peeling, coppery-pink
Bletilla striata (P)	40 cm (16 in)	well drained, sunny	hardy in a warm, sunny situation	8	spring to early summer – 5 to 10 per shoot, purple	ribbed, arching, sword-shaped, 40 to 60 cm (18 to 24 in)	
Buddleja colvilei 'Kewensis' (S)	6 m (20 ft) +	well drained; open	fairly hardy, needs winter protection in cold areas	8	summer – large, funnel-shaped, rose-pink or crimson	bold, long-tapered, 30 cm (12 in)	
Carex elata 'Bowles' Golden (P)	76 cm (30 in)	moist but not inundated; open	hardy	5	summer – greenish	narrow, arching and drooping leaves, golden, spring to autumn	
Carpinus cordata (T)	8 m (25 ft)	most; open	hardy	4	spring – yellow catkins	heart-shaped, 6.5 cm (2½ in) to 13.5cm (5 in)	Bark: rough, grey and brown

Plant name (description)	Average height	Soil and situation (ideally)	Hardiness UK	Hardiness Zone, North America	Flowers	Leaves (deciduous unless otherwise indicated)	Fruits, bark etc.
Chusquea couleou (P) (bamboo)	5 m (16 ft)	fertile, well drained; open	hardy except in severe winter	9		evergreen, narrow, slender–pointed, 7 cm (2¾ in) in dense tufts	Canes: solid, rather than hollow, deep olive green
Cistus populifolius (S)	1 to 2 m (3 to 6 ft)	well drained, prefers neutral or acid soil in sun	relatively hardy except in cold areas	7	early summer – white, with yellow eye	evergreen, heart-shaped, 9 cm (3½ in) long	
Clethra delavayi (S)	4 to 6 m (12 to 20 ft)	lime-free, moist, but well drained open but sheltered	needs winter protection in cold areas	8	mid summer – cup-shaped, 1.5 cm (½ in) wide, dense, creamy-white spikes	dark green, lance-shaped, 10 to 15 cm (4 to 6 in)	
Cornus alternifolia 'Argentea' (S)	4.5 m (15 ft)	most; open	hardy	3	early summer – tiny, yellowish-white	small, alternate, variegated – green and white	attractive tabulated growth
Cornus controversa 'Variegata' (T)	10 to 15 m (32 to 55 ft)	moist, but well drained, in sunny, sheltered site	hardy	5	summer – white, small	small, variegated	distinct, tabulated growth
Cornus kousa var. chinensis (T)	6 to 9 m (20 to 30 ft) fast growing	moist, but well drained, sun or partial shade	hardy	5	summer – creamy-white bracts, star-shaped	colouring well in autumn	Fruit: round, fleshy, red, in autumn
Crinum x powellii (P) (bulb)	1.2 m (4 ft)	moist; but well drained; open	hardy except in cold areas	7	summer – on stems up to 1.2 m (4 ft), trumpet-shaped, rose-pink or white	long, fleshy, strap-shaped	
Daphne bholua 'Gurkha' (S)	2 m (6 ft)	moist, but well drained and lime-free, open	prefers woodland site or sheltered wall	9	winter – white, flushed rose-purple, in clusters	long, pointed, glossy green	
Davidia involucrata (T)	20 m (65 ft)	most, deep loam preferred, open	hardy, prefers some shelter	6	late spring – large white bracts	heart-shaped	Fruit: late summer

Plant	Height	Soil/Conditions	Hardiness	Zone	Flowers	Leaves	Fruit
Decaisnea fargesii (S)	4 to 5 m (13 to 16 ft)	most, prefers rich loam; open	hardy	5	summer – yellowish-green, drooping heads	60 cm to 1 m (2 to 3 ft), long, much divided	Fruit: like pods of broad beans, leaden-blue
Dictamnus albus var. purpureus (P)	1 m (3 ft)	fertile, well drained	hardy, prefers sun or partial shade	2	early summer – long-stalked, 5-petalled, purple	divided, aroma of lemon peel	
Dregea sinensis (CL)	3 to 4 m (9 to 13 ft)	well drained, sunny, dry conditions	hardy except in cold areas	8	summer – star-like, fragrant, creamy-white	slender, pointed, heart-shaped	
Drimys winteri var. andina (S)	1.5 m (5 ft)	prefers acid or neutral soil, moist but well drained open	hardy except in cold areas	9	summer – white, fragrant, 2.5 to 3 cm (1 to 1¼ in) across, clusters	evergreen, fleshy	
Dryopteris wallichiana (P) (fern)	1.5 m (5 ft)	moist in shade or partial shade	hardy	5		dark, shining green, leathery fronds on rich brown scaly stalks	
Elaeagnus angustifolia var. caspica (S)	3 to 4.5 m (10 to 15 ft)	most but preferably well drained in sun; open	hardy, salt tolerant	2	early summer – tiny, silvery scaly outside, yellow within, scented	5 cm (2 in) long, silvery	
Embothrium coccineum (T)	9 m (30 ft) +	acid, moist but well drained	relatively hardy, needs sun and shelter	9	late spring to early summer – red, tubular, crowded	semi-deciduous, lance-shaped	
Epimedium acuminatum (P)	60 cm (2 ft)	moist, but well drained in sun or shade	hardy in sheltered site	7	spring – 4 to 5 cm (1½ to 2 in), purple and white with long spurs	lance-shaped, slender, pointed	
Eryngium giganteum (P)	1 m (3 ft)	well drained, fertile	hardy, prefers full sun or light shade	8	summer – dense, teasel-like, pale blue	luminous, silvery, leathery, toothed	
Erysimum 'Bowles' Mauve' (P)	60 to 90 cm (2 to 3 ft)	most soils, well drained; open	not reliably hardy	8	mainly in spring – mauve-purple, 4-petalled	long, narrow, grey-green	

Plant name (description)	Average height	Soil and situation (ideally)	Hardiness UK	Hardiness Zone, North America	Flowers	Leaves (deciduous unless otherwise indicated)	Fruits, bark etc.
Eucalyptus niphophila (T)	9 m (30 ft)	lime-free, well drained sunny, open site	hardy except in coldest areas	9	summer – petal-less, numerous, white clusters	evergreen, large, lance-shaped	Bark: smooth, piebald
Eurphorbia mellifera (S)	4.5 m (15 ft)	most, well drained	needs winter protection in colder areas	9	spring – clusters of brown and green, honey-scented	evergreen, long and narrow	
Euphorbia wallichii (P)	75 cm(2½ ft)	moist, but well drained; open but sheltered	protect from frost	8	late spring to early summer – large yellow heads	7.5 to 12 cm (3 to 5 in), tapered, pale mid-rib	
Fothergilla gardenii (S)	1 m (3 ft)	lime-free, acid, sandy loam best; open	hardy	5	late spring – fragrant, long white stamens in dense, thimble-sized heads	small leathery, 6 cm (2½ in) long, autumn colours superb	
Glaucidium palmatum (P)	1 to 1.2 m (3 to 4 ft) eventually	moist, well drained, partial shade, sheltered from wind	hardy	6	late spring – lavender poppy-like, single, 5 to 8 cm (2 to 3 in), 4 petals	lobed, sharply toothed, 20 cm (8 in) across	
Hamamelis vernalis 'Sandra' (S)	3 m (10 ft)	acid to neutral, preferably in sun; open	hardy	4	winter – deep yellow	colourful in autumn with orange, purple, flame and crimson tints	
Hacquetia epipactis (P)	10 to 15 cm (4 to 6 in)	fertile, moist, but well drained, partial shade	hardy	6	spring – tiny, yellow with collar of yellow-green bracts	clover-shaped, bright green	
Hebe hulkeana (S)	1 m (3 ft)	most, well drained, sunny position	requires winter protection in cold areas	9	early summer – small, 1 cm (1/3 in) numerous, plumes of pale violet	evergreen, leathery, finely toothed 2.5 to 5 cm (1 to 2 in)	

Name	Height	Soil	Hardiness	Zone	Flowers	Foliage	Notes
Hydrangea quercifolia (S)	1.5 m (5 ft)	moist, but well drained, fertile, prefers sun or partial shade	hardy	5	summer to early autumn – dense, conical, 20 to 25 cm (8 to 10 in) long, white florets	large, boldly lobed, often colouring in autumn	
Indigofera heterantha (S)	1 m (3 ft) +	well drained, full sun	hardy, except in cold areas	8	summer – small, purple, in clusters, 7.5 to 12.5 cm (3 to 5 in) long	small, numerous leaflets	
Juniperus conferta (Co)	prostrate	most, salt tolerant	hardy	5		needle-like, pale, glossy, evergreen	
Lapageria rosea (Cl)	4.5 m (15 ft) +	moist, but well drained in shade	hardy, except in cold areas	9	summer – rich crimson	glossy, dark green, slender, pointed	
Lathraea clandestina (P)	7.5 cm (3 in)	most, preferably moist in shade	hardy	6	spring – flowers in clusters, purple	leafless parasite	
Leycesteria crocothyrsos (S)	2 m (6 ft)	well drained, warm, sunny position	tender	9	summer – yellow, tubular, in drooping tassels	paired, green, slender, 15 cm (6 in) long	Fruit: like soft gooseberries
Liquidambar formosana (T)	12 to 15 m (40 to 50 ft)	preferably lime-free	relatively hardy	6		bold, 3-lobed, good autumn colour	
Lobelia tupa (P)	2 m (6 ft)	fertile, moist but well drained in sun and shelter	hardy except in cold areas	9	summer – reddish-scarlet, in long racemes	lance-shaped, light green, downy	
Lychnis x haageana (P)	30 to 45 cm (12 to 18 in)	most, well drained in full sun	hardy	2	summer – large, scarlet	downy, green or bronze	
Magnolia campbellii (T)	20 m (65 ft) +	deep; lime-free loam, moist, but well drained	relatively hardy, flowers susceptible to frost	7	late winter – pink or rose-coloured	large	
Magnolia cylindrica (T)	6 m (20 ft)	lime-free, moist, but well drained	hardy, prefers shelter	6	spring – cylindrical, erect, creamy-white	bold, bronze-tinted when young	

Plant name (description)	Average height	Soil and situation (ideally)	Hardiness UK	Hardiness Zone, North America	Flowers	Leaves (deciduous unless otherwise indicated)	Fruits, bark etc.
Magnolia liliflora 'Nigra' (S)	4 m (13 ft)	moist, but well drained, lime-free, open	hardy	5	mid spring to early summer – purple outside, white clouded purple inside; one of the longest flowering magnolias	dark green, glossy topped	
Magnolia 'Wada's Memory' (T)	9 m (30 ft)	lime-free, moist, but well drained; open	hardy	4	spring – white, multi-petalled, lax or drooping	narrow oval to lance-shaped, reddish when young	
Mahonia nervosa (S)	30 to 40 cm (12 to 16 in)	lime-free, moist, but well drained, partial shade	hardy	5	spring – small, yellow, cup-shaped, crowded into racemes 15 to 20 cm (6 to 8 in)	45 cm (18 in) long, firm, leathery, red in autumn, 2 rows of leaflets	Fruit: follows flowers, blue-black
Malus transitoria (T)	6 m (20 ft)	most, open	hardy	5	late spring – white, pink-tinted in bud, borne in clusters along the branches	small, neat, glossy green, deeply lobed, toothed; good autumn colour	Fruit: yellow, pea-sized, last to winter
Melianthus major (P)	2 m (6 ft)	fertile, well drained, warm, sunny site	relatively hardy except in cold areas	9	summer – brownish-red	large, deeply divided, blue-green	
Microbiota decussata (Co)	50 cm (21 in) wide spreading to several m	most; open	hardy	2		paired; summer – bright green, winter – purple-brown	Excellent ground cover
Morina longifolia (P)	60 cm (2 ft)	moist, but well drained; open	hardy	5	summer – dense whorls white become rose then crimson	evergreen, strap-shaped, spine toothed	

Name	Height	Soil/Situation	Hardiness	Zone	Flowers	Leaves	Other features
Mutisia oligodon (Cl)	2 m (6 ft)	well drained, warm and sunny	relatively hardy except in cold areas	9	summer to autumn 5 to 7.5 cm (2 to 3 in) salmon-pink petals	stalkless, coarsely toothed, 4 cm (1½ in) long, long tendrils	
Myrtus luma (T)	9 to 12 m (30 to 40 ft)	prefers neutral or acid, in sun or partial shade	tender	9	late summer to early autumn – numerous, small, white	evergreen, small, dark green, leathery	Bark: piebald, flaky; Fruit: small, black, fleshy, edible
Nicotiana sylvestris (B or short-lived P)	1.4 m (5 ft)	not too rich, preferably in partial shade	hardy, except in cold areas	8	late summer to early autumn – white, long-tubed, nodding, 9 cm (3½ in), fragrant	large, green	
Nyssa sinensis (T)	6 m (20 ft) +	prefers moist, lime-free open	hardy in sheltered site	7		summer – green, glossy; best in autumn – yellow, red, 15 cm (6 in) long	
Ozothamnus rosmarinifolius (S)	2 m (6 ft)	well drained, prefers acid and sun	tender	8	summer – white, striking red when in bud	evergreen, needle-like	dense rounded habit when young
Paeonia suffruticosa 'Joseph Rock' (S)	1 to 1.2 m (3 to 4 ft)	good drainage essential sun	hardy, risk of damage from late frost	5	summer – large, white with maroon centre	deeply divided	
Pancratium illyricum (P)	45 cm (18 in)	well drained, in full sun	not very hardy	9	late spring to early summer – white, 6 to 9 cm (2 to 4 in)	strap-shaped	
Photinia villosa var. maximowicziana (S)	5 m (16 ft)	neutral or acid, well drained in sun	hardy	4	late spring – small, white, clustered	splendid autumn colour, leathery, veined	Fruit: autumn, orange-red
x Phylliopsis hillieri 'Pinocchio' (S)	30 cm (12 in)	cool, peaty, well drained, sun or partial shade	hardy	6	late spring – bell-shaped, red-purple	evergreen, narrow	

Plant name (description)	Average height	Soil and situation (ideally)	Hardiness UK	Hardiness Zone, North America	Flowers	Leaves (deciduous unless otherwise indicated)	Fruits, bark etc.
Picea breweriana (Co)	15 to 20 m (50 to 65 ft)	moist, but well drained, in sun open	hardy	4		needle-like on weeping branchlets	Cones: cigar-shaped, 6 to 10 cm (3 to 4 in) long, green changing to purple then brown
Pinus aristata (Co)	6 m (20 ft) +	most; open	hardy	4		closely packed needles with white resin flecks; densely branched	Cones: with bristle-tipped scales
Pinus bungeana (Co)	9 to 12 m (30 to 40 ft) +	most, well drained	hardy	4		light green needles	beautiful marbled bark
Prostanthera cuneata (S)	1 m (3 ft)	well drained, in sun or partial shade	relatively hardy	9	summer – bell-shaped, 2-lipped, 2 cm (¾ in) across, white	evergreen, tiny, dark green, dense, smelling of wintergreen when bruised	
Rhododendron bureavii (S)	3 m (9 ft)	acid open or partial shade	hardy	4	late spring – tubular bell-shaped, white or rose in trusses	handsome leaves, 7.5 to 12.5 cm (3 to 5 in) long, glossy, richly coloured beneath	attractive young growths
Rhododendron macabeanum (S)	6 m (20 ft)	acid open	hardy	8	early spring – dense trusses, tubular bell-shaped, 7.5 cm (3 in), ivory-white to yellow	large, leathery, 30 cm (12 in) long	attractive young growths
Robinia hispida (S)	3 m (9 ft) best against support	well drained, warm, sunny site	hardy, should be sheltered from winds	5	early summer – like small, rose sweet peas in clusters	dark green, with many leaflets	Stems: thornless, young shoots are red bristly

Name	Height	Soil/Position	Hardiness	Zone	Flower	Leaf	Notes
Rodgersia pinnata (P)	1 m (3 ft)	moist, preferably in sun or partial shade	hardy	5	summer – pyramidal plumes, tiny, crowded, pinkish-white	bold, divided, leathery	
Rosa bracteata (Cl or S)	3m (10ft) +	well drained, warm, sunny position	mild areas only	9	summer and autumn – 10 cm (4 in) across, white, single	evergreen, dark and glossy	fiercely thorny
Rosa moyesii 'Geranium' (S)	2.5 to 3 m (7 to 9 ft)	most, full sun	hardy	5	early summer – blood red with creamy stamens, 5 to 6.5 cm (2 to 2½ in) across	7–13 leaflets, toothed	Fruit scarlet, bottle-shaped, in autumn
Roscoea auriculata (P)	40 cm (16 in)	cool, moist, well drained, humus-rich, sun or partial shade	hardy	8	late summer to / early autumn – long-tubed, orchid-like, purple	bold green, lance-shaped	
Rubus biflorus (S)	2 to 3 m (6 to 9 ft)	most; open	hardy	7		divided into several leaflets	Stems: thorny, blue-white in winter
Sanguinaria canadensis 'Flore Pleno' (P)	10 cm (4 in)	moist, but well drained, sun or partial shade	hardy	3	fully double	spring – blue-grey, kidney-shaped	blood-red sap in root
Sassafras albidum (T)	15 to 18 m (40 to 50 ft)	moist, but well drained open	hardy	4		thin in texture, 15 cm (6 in) long, shape variable, autumn colour is eye-catching	Bark: dark, reddish-brown, furrowed
Saxifraga umbrosa (P)	30 cm (12 in)	most; open or partial shade	hardy	6	late spring/early summer – small, starry, white with red stain	leathery, toothed, spoon-shaped	excellent ground cover

Plant name (description)	Average height	Soil and situation (ideally)	Hardiness UK	Hardiness Zone, North America	Flowers	Leaves (deciduous unless otherwise indicated)	Fruits, bark etc.
Sisyrinchium douglasii (P)	20 to 25 cm (8 to 10 in)	moist, but well drained; open	hardy	8	early spring – nodding, bell-shaped, 1.5 to 2 cm (½ to ¾ in) long, reddish-purple	rush-like	
Solanum crispum 'Glasnevin' (Cl)	9 m (30 ft)	most, well drained, warm, sunny	not hardy in cold areas, needs sun and warmth	8	summer to autumn – royal blue with yellow stamens	evergreen	
Sorbus cashmiriana (T)	6 to 9 m (20 to 30 ft)	most; open	hardy	4	spring – dense clusters, white with slight pink blush	bold, divided, russet and gold in autumn	Fruit: marble-sized, green turning white from autumn to Christmas
Sorbus wardii (T)	9 m (30ft)	most; open	hardy	4	late spring – small, white few flowered clusters	broadly oval; rounded, 12.5 cm (15 in) long, ribbed, parallel veins	Fruit: follows flowers, substantial, yellow ripening to brown
Stipa gigantea (P) (grass)	2.5 m (8 ft)	good drainage, full sun	hardy	6	late summer – golden then straw-yellow	long, narrow, green	
Styrax hemsleyana (T)	6 to 9 m (20 to 30 ft)	deep, moist, well drained, lime-free, sheltered, sunny site	hardy	7	early summer – white, bell-shaped, 2.5 cm (1in) across in racemes	large, to 14 cm (5½ in) long, good autumn colour	
Thalictrum delavayi (P)	1.5m (5 ft)	rich, deep soil, sun, shelter	hardy	8-9	summer – pale violet, cream stamens	dainty, much divided	
Tropaeolum speciosum (Cl)	7m (22 ft)	moist, but well drained acid or peaty soil	hardy in wetter western and southern areas	9	late summer – scarlet, yellow throat	emerald green, rounded, deeply divided	Fruit: green to rich indigo

	Height	Soil	Hardiness		Flowering	Notes
Veratrum album (P)	2 m (6 ft)	cool, deep, rich soil, sun or partial shade	hardy	4	late summer – greenish-white, 6-petalled, dense spikes	large, bold veins
Viola 'Jackanapes' (P)	23 cm (9 in)	moist, but well drained, prefers light shade	hardy	5	late spring to summer – lower petals yellow, upper brown	beloved of slugs
Watsonia beatricis (P)	1 m (3 ft)	moist, but well drained, sun	hardy except in cold areas	9	summer to early autumn – funnel-shaped, apricot	evergreen, iris-like
Xanthoceras sorbifolium (T or S)	3 to 5 m (9 to 15 ft)	well drained, full sun	hardy	4	late spring – 2.5 to 3 cm (1 to 1¼ in), white with yellow stains	divided, sharply toothed; Fruit: large capsules on drooping stalks
Zauschneria cana (P)	45 cm (18 in)	well drained, full sun	needs protection in winter	9	summer and autumn – slender, scarlet	grey, narrow

Recommended Reading

Gardeners, no matter how experienced, or how retentive their memories, must at times have recourse to reference books and the experiences of others. There are a myriad of books available to the keen gardener on subjects general as well as specific. One cannot buy them all so a selection has to be made. Here are some of the books that have served me well over the years and that as a plantsman I would not be without.

Trees and Shrubs Hardy in the British Isles by W. J. Bean, 8th edition (revised)
Four volumes and a supplement in the offing. Expensive but for those interested in woody plants indispensible. Not for nothing is it known as the tree and shrub enthusiast's bible.

Hilliers Manual of Trees and Shrubs
This has been called by some a mini Bean. Brief descriptions of over 8,000 woody plants, ideal for the gardener's pocket or bag.

Ingwersen's Manual of Alpine Plants
An Alpine plant version of Hilliers' Manual written by the Old Master himself, Will Ingwersen.

The Bulb Book by Martyn Rix and Roger Phillips
Outstanding for its colour photographs of a wide range of bulbs both rare and well known, easy to use and with brief but practical descriptions and notes on cultivation.

The Peat Garden and its Plants by Alfred Evans
An authoritative and practical account of a surprisingly wide range of hardy plants.

Perennial Garden Plants by Graham Stuart Thomas
Still the best general guide to perennials for British and American gardens. Written by the authority on the subject.

American Gardens – A Traveller's Guide Brooklyn Botanic Gardens Publication Vol. 42, No. 3
A new and updated edition of this handy guide first published in 1970. Some 250 gardens are featured. Includes both colour and black and white photographs.

The Field Guide to the Trees of Britain and Northern Europe by Alan Mitchell
Still the best of its kind for those keen on identifying trees. Rumour has it that an American version is forthcoming. Hurray!

The Cultivation of New Zealand Trees and Shrubs by L. J. Metcalf
The best account on its subject, highly practical.

Australian Native Plants by J. W. Wrigley and M. Fagg
For those able to grow these plants (lucky Californians) this book offers an excellent practical account.

Encyclopaedia of Australian Plants by W. R. Elliot and D. L. Jones
Four volumes published with more to come. Expensive but invaluable. Comprehensive and well illustrated in colour.

Manual of Woody Landscape Plants by Michael Dirr
A highly original and eminently practical account for American gardeners. Full of common sense, experience and refreshing touches of humour.

Plants that Merit Attention by The Garden Club of America
Volume 1: *Trees* is already published with more to come. If *Trees* is anything to go by this will become a classic reference of its kind for American gardeners with lessons for British gardeners too. Well designed and illustrated.

The Vanishing Garden by Christopher Brickell and Fay Sharman
For those who wonder what the conservation of garden plants is all about this is the book for you. It is packed with information on choice plants, many of them rare and unusual.

Collins Guide to the Pests, Diseases and Disorders of Garden Plants by Stefan Buczacki and Keith Harris
For those who want to know what is wrong with their ailing plants, this book is hard to beat; a real chamber of horrors, it does however offer a ray of hope in methods of treatment, etc.

The Oxford Companion to Gardens by Geoffrey and Susan Jellicoe, Patrick Goode and Michael Lancaster
A most comprehensive account of the design and history of the world's gardens. Over 700 examples featured and well illustrated.

List of Plant Sources

T = Trees S = Shrubs and Climbers C = Conifers
P = Perennials and Others

Britain and Ireland

The following is merely a selection of plant sources offering interesting plants to the keen gardener. A far more comprehensive account is *The Plant Finder*, a recent publication from The Hardy Plant Society.

Mr. K. Ashburner, Stone Lane Gardens, Stone Farm, Chagford, Devon TQ13 8JU (T)

David Austin Roses, Bowling Green Lane, Albrighton WV7 3HB (Roses)

Ballalheannagh Gardens, Glen Roy, Lonan, Isle of Man (S,C,P)

F. G. Barcock & Co. Ltd, Garden House Farm, Drinkstone, Bury St. Edmunds, Suffolk IP30 9TN (T,S,P)

Peter Beales, Intwood Nurseries, Swardeston, Norwich NR14 8EA (Roses)

Bluebell Nurseries, Blackfordby, Nr. Burton-on-Trent, Staffordshire DE11 8AJ (T,S,C,P)

Bressingham Gardens, Diss, Norfolk, IP22 2AB (S,C,P)

Broadleigh Gardens, Barr House, Bishops Hull, Taunton, Somerset TA4 1AE (Bulbs)

Burncoose and Southdown Nurseries, Gwennap, Redruth, Cornwall TR16 6BJ (T,S,P)

Careby Manor Gardens, Careby, Stamford, Lincolnshire PE9 4EA (P)

Mr. P. Chappell, Spinners, Boldre, Lymington, Hampshire (T,S,P)

Chiltern Seeds, Bortree Stile, Ulverston, Cumbria LA12 7BP (T,S,P, seeds)

County Park Nursery, Essex Gardens, Hornchurch, Essex (S,P)

The Dairies (James Russell), Castle Howard, York, Yorkshire (T,S,C)

Edrom Nurseries, Coldingham, Eyemouth, Berwickshire TD14 5TZ (S,P)

English Eucalyptus, Blue Gums Garden Centre, The Quarter, Lamberhurst, Kent TN3 BAL (Eucalypts)

Fernhill Nursery, Sandyford, Co. Dublin, Ireland (T,S,C,P)

The Fortescue Garden Trust, The Garden House, Buckland Monachorum, Yelverton, Devon PL20 7LQ (T,S,P)

Fyne Trees, Cairdow, Argyll (T,C)

Glendoick Gardens Ltd, Glendoick, Perth, Scotland PH2 7NS (S)

Goldbrook Plants, Hoxne, Eye, Suffolk (S,P)

Goscote Nurseries Ltd, Syston Road, Cossington, Leicestershire LE7 8N7 (T,S)

Green Farm Plants, Green Farm, Bentley, Farnham, Surrey (S,P)

Hillier Nurseries (Winchester) Ltd, Ampfield House, Ampfield, Romsey, Hampshire SO5 9PA (T,S,C,P)

Holden Clough Nursery, Holden, Bolton-By-Bowland, Clitheroe, Lancashire BB7 4PF (S,C,P)

Hopleys Plants, High Street, Much Hadham, Hertfordshire (S,P)

Hydon Nurseries, Clockbarn Lane, Hydon Heath, Nr. Godalming, Surrey GU8 4AZ (S)

W. E. Th. Ingwersen Ltd., Birch Farm Nursery, Gravetye, East Grinstead, West Sussex RH19 4LE (S,C,P)

Reginald Kaye Ltd., Waithman Nurseries, Silverdale, Carnforth, Lancashire LA5 0TY (S,C,P)

Knightshayes Garden Trust, Knightshayes Court, Tiverton, Devon (T,S,C,P)

The Knoll Gardens (John May), Stapehill Road, Stapehill, Wimborne, Dorset BH21 7ND (S)

Longstock Park Nursery, Longstock Park, Stockbridge, Hampshire SO20 6EH (S,P)

Mallet Court Nursery, Mallet Court, Curry Mallet, Taunton, Somerset TA3 6SY (T,S)

Marwood Hill (Dr. J. Smart), Barnstaple, Devon EX31 4EB (T,S)

Notcutts Nurseries, Woodbridge, Suffolk IP12 4AF (T,S,C,P)

J. & E. Parker-Jervis, Marten's Hall Farm, Longworth, Abingdon, Oxon OX13 5EP (P)

Penwood Nurseries (Mr. & Mrs. D. Harris), Nr. Newbury, Berkshire (T,S,C)

G. Reute Ltd., Jackass Lane, Keston, Kent BR2 6AW (S,C)

Rosemoor Garden Trust, Torrington, Devon EX38 7EG (T,S,C,P)

Savill Garden Plant Centre, Savill Gardens, Windsor, Berkshire (T,S,C,P)

Seaforde Gardens, Seaforde, Co. Down, N. Ireland (T,S,C,P)

Shanahan's Nurseries, Villa Gardens, Clonakilty, Co. Cork (T,S,C)

Sherrards Nursery, Snelsmore Road, Donnington, Newbury, Berkshire (T,S)

Sifelle Nursery, The Walled Garden, Newick Park, Newick, Lewes, East Sussex

Starborough Nursery, Starborough Road, Marsh Green, Edenbridge, Kent TN8 5RB (T,S,C)

Stone House Cottage Nurseries, Stone, Nr. Kidderminster, Worcestershire (S,P)

Treasures of Tenbury, Burford House, Tenbury Wells, Worcestershire (T,S,P)

Tree Seeds of Bamber Ltd, Lower Seed Lee Farm, Brindle Road, Bamber Bridge, Preston, Lancashire PR5 6AP (Maples)

Unusual Plants, (Beth Chatto) White Barn House, Elmstead Market, Colchester, Essex CO7 7DP (P)

Valleyhead Nursery, Dihewyd, Lampeter, Dyfed SA48 7PJ (T,S,C,P)

Wallace & Barr Ltd, Marden, Kent TN12 9BP (P)

The Wansdyke Nurseries, Hillworth, Devizes, Wiltshire SN10 58D (C)

Washfield Nurseries, Horns Road, Hawkhurst, Kent (S,P)

Wisley Plant Sales Centre, R.H.S. Garden, Wisley, Woking, Surrey GU23 6QB (T,S,C,P)

Woodruff Nursery, 176 Rownhams Lane, North Baddesley, Romsey, Hampshire (T,S)

North America

Listed below are a few of the many nurseries supplying new and unusual plants. Far more comprehensive and satisfactory is the *Nursery Source Guide Handbook*, No. 83 obtainable from the Brooklyn Botanic Garden, 1,000 Washington Avenue, Brooklyn, New York 11225.

Gossler Farms Nursery, 1200 Weaver Road, Springfield, Oregon 97478 (T,S)

Monrovia Nursery Co., P.O. Box Q, 18331 East Foothill Blvd., Azusa, CA 91702 (T,S,C)

Siskiyou Rare Plant Nursery, 2825 Cummings Road, Medford, Oregon 97501 (S,P)

Western Hills Nursery, 16250 Coleman Valley Road, Occidental, CA 95465 (T,S,P)

Woodlanders, Inc., 1128 Colleton Avenue, Aiken, S.C. 29801 (T,S,P and Native Plants)

List of Specialist Societies

There are numerous societies and organizations offering services of interest to plant enthusiasts. These include informative publications as well as expert advice and seed schemes. Here are a few of the most pertinent.

Britain and Ireland

Alpine Garden Society, E. M. Upward (Secretary), Lye End Link, St. John's, Woking, Surrey GU21 1SW

British Hosta and Hemerocallis Society, R. M. Kitchingman (Secretary), Pelham, Chideock, Bridport, Dorset DT6 6JW

British Iris Society, G. E. Cassidy (Secretary), 67 Bushwood Road, Kew, Surrey TW9 3BG

British Ivy Society, Fred Kennedy (Secretary), 66 Cornwall Road, Ruislip, Middlesex HA4 6AN

British Pteridological (Fern) Society, A. R. Busby (Secretary), University of Warwick, Dept. of Science Education, Westwood, Coventry CV4 7AL

Hardy Plant Society, Mrs. J. Sambrooke (Secretary), Garden Cottage, 214 Ruxley Lane, West Ewell, Surrey KT17 9EU

International Dendrology Society, Mrs Eustace (Secretary), Whistley Green Farmhouse, Hurst, Reading, Berkshire RG10 0DU

Irish Garden Plant Society, Mrs J. Newell (Secretary), c/o National Botanic Garden, Glasnevin, Dublin 9 or Mr Maxwell, c/o Belfast Parks Dept., Fernhill House, Belfast, N. Ireland

National Council for the Conservation of Plants and Gardens, c/o Wisley Garden, Nr Woking Surrey GU23 6QB

Northern Horticultural Society, R. E. Shersby (Secretary), Harlow Car Gardens, Harrogate HG3 1QB

The Royal Horticultural Society, 80 Vincent Square, Westminster, London SW1P 2PE

Royal Horticultural Society of Ireland, Thomas Prior House, Merrion Road, Ballsbridge, Dublin 4

Scottish Rock Garden Club, Dr Evelyn Stevens (Secretary), Scoltie, Doune Road, Dunblane, Perthshire FK15 9AR

North America

American Horticultural Society, Box 0105, Mount Vernon, VA 2212

The American Ivy Society, PO Box 520, West Carrollton, OH 45449

American Rhododendron Society, 14885, S.W. Sunrise Ln, Tigard, OR 97224

The American Rock Garden Society, Buffy Parker (Secretary), 15 Fairmead Road, Darien, CT 06820

California Horticultural Society, California Academy of Sciences, Golden Gate Park, San Francisco, CA 94118

Los Angeles International Fern Society, PO Box 90943, Pasadena, CA 91109–0943

Strybing Arboretum Society of Golden Gate Park, Ninth Avenue & Lincoln Way, San Francisco, CA 94122

Index